The Classic Instruction Series *from Tennis* Magazine

Tennis
Strokes
and
Strategies

SIMON AND SCHUSTER *New York*

Published by Simon and Schuster
A Division of Gulf & Western Corporation
Simon & Schuster Building
Rockefeller Center
1230 Avenue of the Americas
New York, New York 10020

Designed by Irving Perkins
Manufactured in the United States of America

5   6   7   8   9   10   11   12   13   14

Library of Congress Cataloging in Publication Data

Main entry under title:

Tennis strokes and strategies.

    1. Tennis.   I. Tennis (Highland Park, Ill.)
GV995.T44   796.34′22   75-14065
ISBN 0-671-22073-X

Contents

Introduction

This book grew out of a decision made several years ago at *Tennis* magazine. Before the current tennis "boom" began, the magazine was a good deal smaller than it is today, but we could sense the coming explosion. We sensed, too, that the real future of tennis lay not at Wimbledon or at Forest Hills but in the parks, clubs, indoor centers and resorts across the country. For this reason, we decided to tailor our editorial mix not to tennis *spectators* but to the tennis *player*. The question we asked ourselves then—and the question we continue to ask ourselves at the magazine today—is: what sort of articles should we publish to help tennis players derive maximum enjoyment from the game?

We were especially concerned about instructional material, and this concern led us to formulate the concept of a portfolio of tennis instruction—a self-contained, visually exciting series on a single aspect of the game. The idea was simple: take the backhand, for example, and break it down into explicit categories—technique, strategy, psychology and conditioning. We wanted the portfolios to reflect the knowledge and experience of the game's top professionals in a way that appealed to players of all levels of ability.

Earlier, we had put together a special instructional advisory board made up of established experts whose responsibility was, and is, to coordinate and authenticate all instruction material that appears in the magazine. The panel is composed of Tony Trabert, Vic Seixas, George Lott, Bill Price and Ron Holmberg. The portfolios were written by the game's top stars—from Kramer, Gonzalez and Marble to Laver, Newcombe and Court—and carefully reviewed by this panel, working closely with our editors to ensure that the material in each portfolio was technically sound, yet expressed in terms that any reader could understand.

Tennis Strokes and Strategies is a direct outgrowth of this series. It represents the best of the *Tennis* instructional portfolios, along with the best of the instruction that has appeared in other sections of the magazine. Taking it as a whole, I don't think there has been a more impressive collection of tennis instruction within one book. What two people in the world, for instance, are more qualified to talk about backhand technique than Don Budge and Ken Rosewall, both of whom highlight our section on the backhand? Who is more qualified to talk about forehand technique than Jack Kramer, who opens the section on forehand? And on the list goes: Rod Laver on the topspin lob; Arthur Ashe on the cannonball serve; Dennis Ralston on the forehand volley; John Newcombe on the American twist serve; Jan Kodeš on the return of service—in no other book to date have so many of the top names of tennis revealed as much of themselves and their techniques.

We added something else: a regular feature by the talented young Australian pro John Alexander, whose assignment in each portfolio was to relate each topic to the professional game, pointing out examples that our readers could follow when watching the pros in action either in person or on television. Here again our overriding concern was to provide our readers with information they could use to improve their own tennis and thereby enrich their enjoyment of the game.

Not every tennis expert is necessarily a well-known player. In dealing with strategy, psychology and conditioning, we were able to secure the talents of four eminent contributors. Bob Harman, whose by-line appears on several pieces in *Tennis Strokes and Strategies,* is known throughout the tennis world as a "tennis doctor" whose professional "patients" have included Jack Kramer, Louise Brough and Bobby Riggs. Charles Lundgren and Allen Fox are both psychologists, with professional coaching and playing backgrounds. Harry Hopman, former coach of the Australian Davis Cup team, wrote much of the portfolio on conditioning and is the acknowledged master of this subject.

As you might expect, getting all this material together was no simple task. While the professionals we dealt with were not only willing but eager to talk about tennis and illustrate their techniques, the logistics was frequently awesome. Don Budge's excellent section on the backhand, for instance, required numerous long-distance phone conversations during the editing stage between Budge, who is resident pro six months of the year at Tres Vidas, in Acapulco, Mexico, and our editor Shep Campbell, whose biggest problem was dealing with the Spanish-speaking operators. But these difficulties were minor compared with the phone calls following Jack Kramer to different parts of the world to finalize his forehand article. His travel itinerary is more difficult to follow than Henry Kissinger's.

Some diversity of opinion arises among our authors. This diversity is deliberate. We believe that the variety of approaches contained in this book represents one of its strengths. Anyone who has taken the time to study the styles and techniques of the leading players on the professional tour knows full well that there is no *one* way to hit a forehand or backhand or even to grip the racquet, and this fact is plainly reflected in this book.

One final word about the organization of the book. For the convenience of the reader, the material in *Tennis Strokes and Strategies* is divided into three distinct categories: 1) strokes, 2) strategy and 3) practice and conditioning. We have added a substanial number of new photos. In addition, all of the articles have been carefully re-edited and updated, particularly those which deal with examples from the professional game. My deep appreciation for this goes to contributing editor Barry Tarshis, books editor Cal Brown and the *Tennis* editors Shep Campbell and Jeff Bairstow. It is the sort of book, we feel, that players at every level of the game will want to refer to time and again. We have put it together with this purpose in mind.

ASHER J. BIRNBAUM
Editor-in-Chief, *Tennis* Magazine

PART I
Strokes

Chapter 1 The Grip

How Should You Grip the Racquet?
by Fred Weymuller

Of all the fundamentals of tennis strokes, none is more basic than the way you hold the racquet. Your grip influences the angle of the racquet face, where you meet the ball and, most critically, what happens when the strings make contact.

Grips have been a subject of continuing controversy almost since the inception of tennis. A racquet handle has numerous bevels and edges, and there is more than one way to hold a racquet so that the face is in the position in which you want it to be when it meets the ball. The big question, though, is which grip works best for each individual player on each individual stroke—that is, which grip enables you to hit each stroke with the optimum balance of power and control.

Through the years, a wide variety of grip styles have been used by tournament players, but only three can be described as "basic": the Eastern, the Continental and the Western. Although most pros, myself included, recommend the Eastern forehand and backhand grips for most players, we will be concerned here with the merits and shortcomings of all three.

Gripping Terminology

Before getting into the specifics of each, let's clarify the terminology. Most grip instruction focuses on where the "V" in the hand—the crease between the thumb and the index finger—is located in relation to the

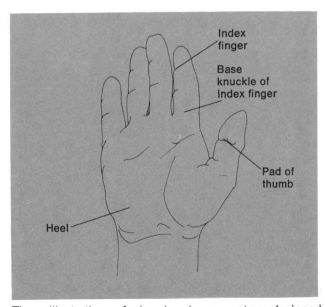

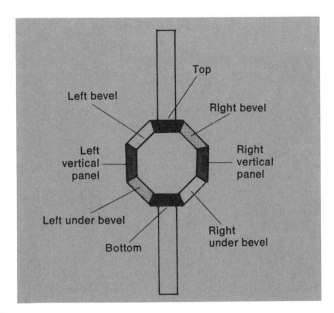

These illustrations of a hand and a racquet are designed to help you as you examine the grips pictured on the next six pages. The key checkpoints of the hand are on the left (#1). On the right (#2) is a diagram of the racquet used in all the following photographs; the view is from behind the butt of the handle looking up toward the head. It shows the eight planes of the handle, which have been covered with colored tape to simplify the identification of each grip.

15

handle. The problem with this approach is that individual hands vary considerably, making the "V" an unreliable reference point. To remedy this problem, I use three checkpoints: the heel of the hand, the base knuckle of the index finger and the thumb pad (see drawing). The directions issued here are meant for right-handers; left-handers should apply them to the opposite side of the handle.

One final introductory word about grip. Regardless of the grip you use, one principle transcends the differences in styles. It is firmness. Unless you hold the racquet firmly enough so that you can feel the pressure of your fingers on the handle, no grip will be effective. Now let's look at the three basic grips of tennis.

The Eastern Grip

There are two Eastern grips: one for the forehand and one for the backhand. The grip itself draws its name from the fact that it first came into wide use on clay courts in the Eastern part of the United States, whose surface normally produces a nice waist-high bounce. Most players favor the Eastern grip over any other because it positions the hand *behind* the racquet handle. This makes the Eastern grip ideal for hitting balls at waist-high level from both the backhand and the forehand. It can easily be adapted for balls that must be met lower or higher. (As we will see, the Continental and Western grips lack this versatility.)

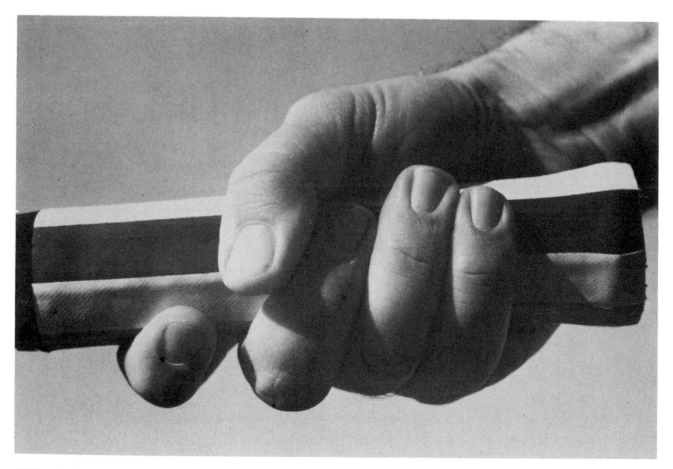

The Eastern Forehand

The Eastern forehand (see illustrations) is sometimes referred to as the "shake hands" grip. You can approximate it by holding the racquet face perpendicular to the ground and then clasping the handle as if you were "shaking hands."

To be more precise: Place the heel of your right hand on the right bevel of the handle and your thumb pad on the left vertical panel. Then close your fingers around the handle (as with most grips, the index finger should be spread slightly away from the other, grouped fingers) with the base knuckle of the index finger resting on the right vertical panel. Practice locating this grip so that you can do it without looking. In a match, you should be watching the ball, not the racquet handle.

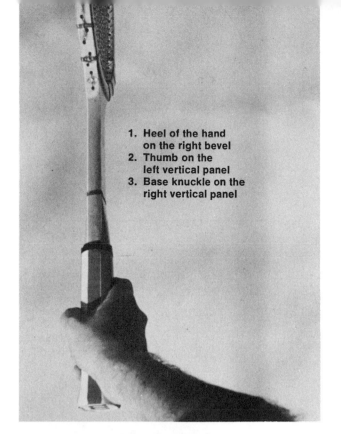

1. Heel of the hand on the right bevel
2. Thumb on the left vertical panel
3. Base knuckle on the right vertical panel

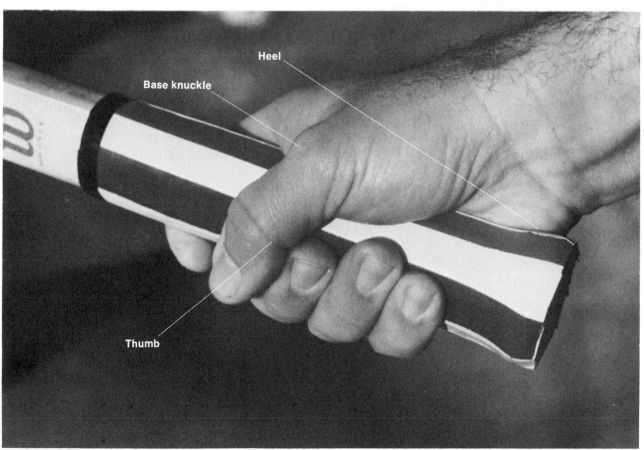

Heel

Base knuckle

Thumb

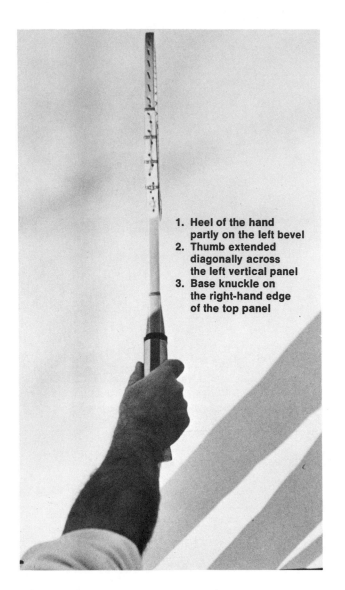

1. **Heel of the hand partly on the left bevel**
2. **Thumb extended diagonally across the left vertical panel**
3. **Base knuckle on the right-hand edge of the top panel**

The Eastern Backhand

To reach the Eastern backhand, rotate the hand about one quarter turn to the left (counterclockwise) from the Eastern forehand. You can tell you're right when the heel of the hand is partly on the left bevel with the rest of the hand protruding off the edges just a bit. Now put the thumb diagonally across the left vertical panel and lay the base knuckle of the forefinger on the right-hand edge of the top panel.

Changing Grips

Although the distance on the racquet handle between the Eastern forehand and backhand is not huge, it is significant enough to require a change each time the ball comes to the opposite side of the body. Changing grips begins in the ready position, with the throat of the racquet in your left hand. Your grip should start to shift just as you begin to draw the racquet back for your shot. The adjustment should be completed well before the racquet has swung back parallel to the body. One good drill you can practice on your own is to stand in front of the mirror, drawing the racquet back and shifting grips to both sides of the body.

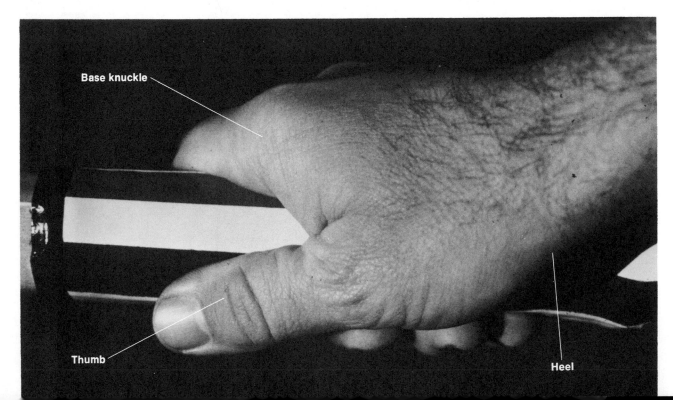

Base knuckle

Thumb

Heel

The Continental Grip

The Continental grip is so named because it originated on the continent of Europe—specifically, in France—where the soft dirt courts produce a low bounce. Unlike the case of the Eastern grip, there is no difference between a forehand Continental and a backhand Continental.

There's no question that the Continental is well suited for handling a low-bouncing ball. It's also adequate for ones that bounce waist high. The trouble comes when balls bounce high. The nature of the grip is such—the palm being on top of the handle—that it's very difficult to gain good racquet-face control on a high ball.

To assume the proper Continental grip, place the racquet lengthwise on its edge in a horizontal position and grasp the handle from above, as if it were a hammer. If you've grasped it correctly, the heel of the hand will be on the top panel, the thumb will be extended straight around the handle and the base knuckle of the forefinger will be on the right bevel.

Although some very successful players—Rod Laver, for one—use the Continental grip for all strokes, it isn't really meant for the average player, with one exception: for vol-

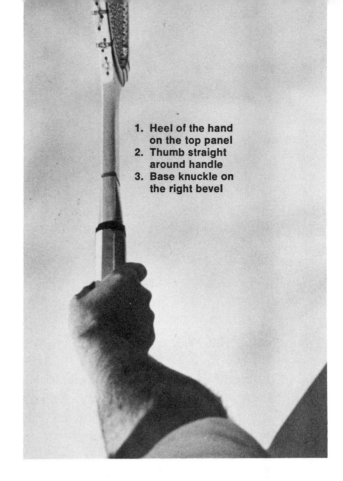

1. Heel of the hand on the top panel
2. Thumb straight around handle
3. Base knuckle on the right bevel

leys. Hitting ground strokes with a Continental grip requires a very strong wrist and more precise timing than is the case with the Eastern grips. These factors, together with the difficulties the grip presents with high balls, are the reason I favor the Eastern grips for average players.

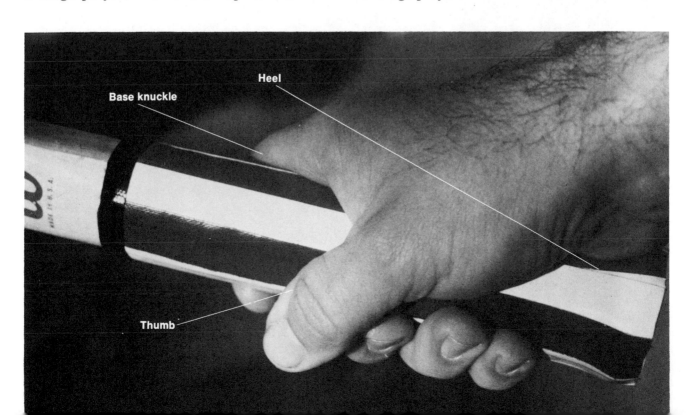

Heel

Base knuckle

Thumb

The Western Grips

The so-called Western grips first developed on the hard cement courts of California, where the ball often bounces high. The grip is well suited for the high ball and is satisfactory for the waist-high ball too. Its problem lies with the low ball. Since the hand is *under* the handle, on both forehand and backhand, it's difficult to get the racquet head down for low balls.

The Western Forehand

To assume the Western forehand, lay the racquet on the floor and grasp it so that the heel of the hand and the base knuckle are on the right under bevel, with the thumb pad on the top panel. There is a variation of this grip—often called the semi-Western—in which the heel and knuckle are on the right vertical panel and the thumb is on the left bevel. This semi-Western grip is probably the most common forehand grip among untutored players.

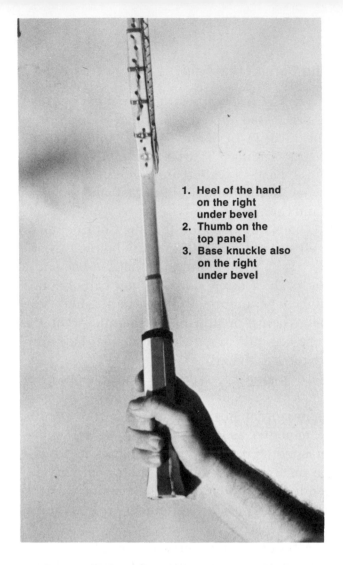

1. Heel of the hand on the right under bevel
2. Thumb on the top panel
3. Base knuckle also on the right under bevel

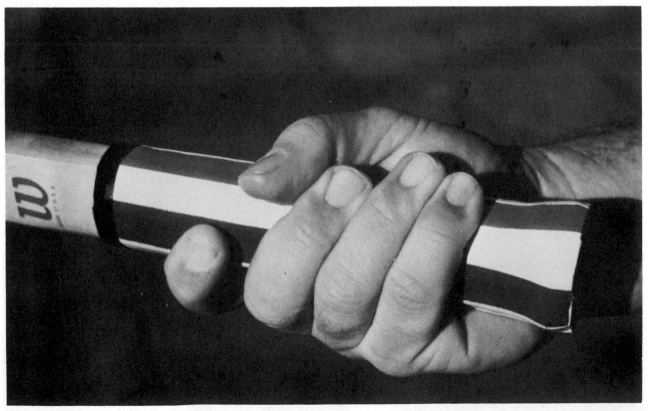

The Western Backhand

Some players who use the Western forehand switch to the backhand by simply turning the racquet upside down and hitting the ball with the same face. Most discover soon enough that an upside-down low backhand is pretty uncomfortable to hit.

Another way is to flip the racquet over and wind up with a Western backhand that is close to the Eastern version: the heel of the hand flush on the left bevel, the thumb straight up the left vertical panel and the base knuckle on the top panel.

Either way, it all gets rather complicated. And that is the problem with the Western grip. It works well enough on high balls to the forehand side, but runs into trouble where change of grip is concerned. In short, I don't recommend the Western grips at all, and neither do most pros.

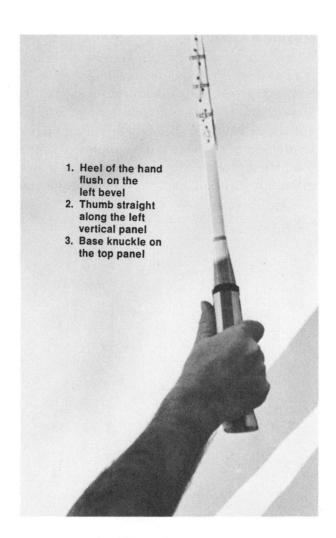

1. Heel of the hand flush on the left bevel
2. Thumb straight along the left vertical panel
3. Base knuckle on the top panel

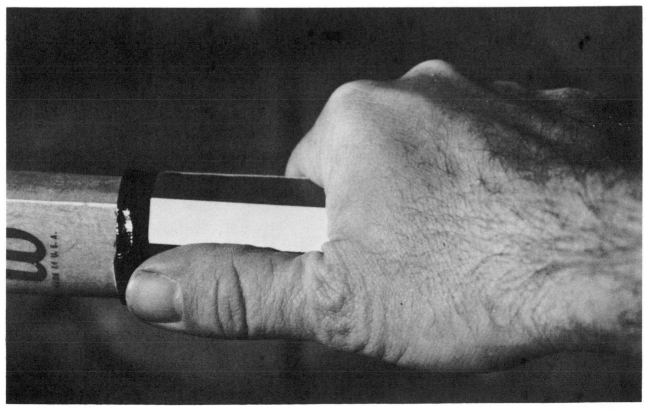

Making a Change

I've already stated my preference for the Eastern grips and given my reasons. But should you change to the Eastern grips if you are using another? If you are young or relatively new to the game, have plenty of time to practice and are willing to work, then a shift, although difficult at first, will probably pay off for you in the long run. On the other hand, if you've been playing tennis for years, and if you're generally satisfied with the results you've been getting with your present grip, then changing probably isn't worthwhile. It will take thousands of practice shots before you begin feeling comfortable with any new grip, and it's probably not worth the trouble.

The Proper Grip Size for You
by Robert P. Nirschl, M.D.

Regardless of which grip style you use—Eastern, Continental or Western—you will still have problems stroking the ball properly unless you have a racquet with the proper grip size for you. If the grip is too big you'll have trouble holding on to the racquet, especially on very hot days when your hands sweat. Too small a grip, on the other hand, can produce blisters.

For years, sporting-goods store salesmen and pro-shop assistants have fitted grips mainly on the basis of trial and error, asking you how a particular grip "feels." In some places, the method is a little more "scientific." You hear criteria such as "touching the seventh octagon of the handle," or "the thumb overlaps the third finger."

There is a simpler, more accurate way to check grip size, one that anyone can easily check himself. It's by means of the palm-crease factor.

Look at the palm of your hand. Notice the lateral creases. The bottom crease, running along the middle portion of the hand, is the one you want. If you take a ruler (see drawing) and measure from the tip of your ring finger to a point on the crease between the ring and middle fingers, you should be able to determine the grip you need. If the measurement comes out to, say, 4½ inches, that is the correct grip size for you.

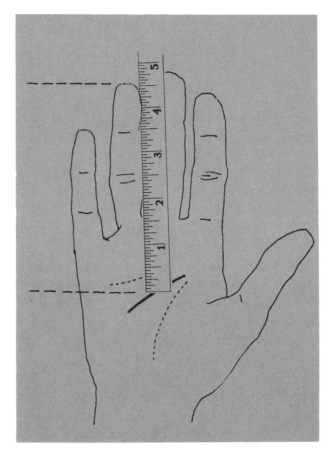

If you're a man, chances are your grip will measure between 4½ and 4¾ inches. The average woman's grip falls between 4⅛ and 4⅜ inches. Children's grips, of course, run smaller.

If you find that the grip you're using now is too big or too small, the adjustment can be made easily and inexpensively at any good tennis shop. And when you go to get the grip adjusted, tell the pro about this technique. You'll be doing the next customer a favor.

What Grips the Pros Use
by John Alexander

It sometimes seems that there have been as many different grips as there have been tennis champions. That's because at the upper reaches of tournament play every player seems to have his own gripping idiosyncrasy—a slight variation from the norm somewhere along the line.

No surprise, then, that very few of the top touring professionals use what might be considered the classic grip—the Eastern forehand and backhand. In fact, many leading players use only one grip for all shots; or if they change for forehands and backhands, the adjustment is a very small one.

Rod Laver has achieved his phenomenal success with only a very slight change from the Continental grip for the forehand to a grip midway between the Continental and the Eastern backhand for his backhand. Many of the Australian players tend to favor a grip that might be described as Continental with little or no change between backhand and forehand.

On the other hand, many American players seem to favor larger grip changes. Stan Smith used to have a pronounced grip change, although recently he seems to be using what is sometimes called the Australian forehand (that is, a grip midway between the Continental and the Eastern forehand) and the Eastern backhand. I use a similar grip change myself, although sometimes—on return of serve, for example—there just isn't enough time to change grips.

I am rather different from most of the pros in that I wait for service with a modified fore-hand grip—like the Australian forehand. Most players wait with their backhand grip, since they anticipate that the serve will be directed at their backhands. Most of the time I prefer to wait with my forehand, because I would rather compromise on my backhand than on my forehand. I find it easier to slice the ball back with an incorrect grip on the backhand than to hit the ball with the wrong grip on the forehand.

Ken Rosewall also waits for serve with a forehand grip. He notes that when you take the racquet back for the backhand, you have to use two hands, which makes it easy to turn the racquet and adjust the grip. By contrast, only one hand is used for the backswing on the forehand, which makes it more difficult to turn the racquet for a grip change.

Several leading women players also seem to favor the single grip. Margaret Court has a modified Eastern forehand grip that, unfortunately, imposes some weakness on her backhand. She has a resulting tendency to slice her backhand all the time, and her grip makes it almost impossible for her to produce a topspin backhand. An extremely pronounced Continental grip is used by Evonne Goolagong—who consequently has a very weak forehand. Unlike these Australian stars, Billie Jean King changes between a modified Eastern forehand and a pure Eastern backhand, which may account for her almost equally good forehand and backhand ground strokes.

Very few top players use the Western grip nowadays. Harold Solomon of the United

Many top stars overcome the deficiencies of unorthodox grips because they have developed great stroke-making ability. Jimmy Connors (above) favors a grip that resembles the Western but is rarely seen today. Evonne Goolagong Cawley (right) has a modified Continental grip that can be used for both backhands and forehands, while Françoise Durr (below) uses a bizarre forehand grip for almost all her strokes.

States and Sweden's Björn Borg both use exaggerated Eastern forehand grips that tend toward the Western. Borg also employs a lot of wrist in order to put topspin on the ball. Jimmy Connors too has a forehand grip close to a Western. However, he has an unusually shaped wrist, which makes it rather difficult to be specific about his grip.

Many players have grips that are very deceptive. Roy Emerson, for example, appears to have a Continental grip for both forehand and backhand. But his wrist is cocked in such an unusual position that he is probably using an Eastern forehand grip.

The strangest grip of all is used by French star Françoise Durr, who has a very bizarre Eastern forehand grip for every shot. Her wrist and elbow lead on her backhand, which is normally a very difficult way to hit a powerful backhand. And the shot does look most peculiar. But she moves into position very well, gets her racquet back quickly and watches the ball very closely. As a result, she has a very effective backhand despite her awkward-looking grip.

It is rare to find a touring pro who will alter his or her grip positions unless there is a fairly obvious weakness in a particular stroke. Cliff Drysdale of South Africa used to have a weak forehand, in part because of the Continental grip he employed. He modified his grip toward the Eastern forehand in 1971 and, partly because of that change, had his best year ever. Unfortunately, he seems to have reverted to the Continental on his forehand.

The chances are that a pro who uses grips other than the classic Eastern forehand and backhand does it because he feels most comfortable with his own grip and has learned to master any of its possible deficiencies. That does not mean that the average player should emulate, for example, a Continental grip simply because Ilie Nastase has been so successful with it. Until his strokes are thoroughly grooved, the average player is probably better off with the Eastern grips.

Chapter 2 The Forehand

Hitting the Power Forehand
by Jack Kramer

How many times have you heard a coach or instructor say, "Never copy anybody else's style"? Well, I think that is bad advice. What is wrong with imitating somebody else—especially if he's a proven success?

When I was a kid in southern California during the 1930's, my hero was Ellsworth Vines. Vines had a classic stroke that really caught my fancy. He was a tall fellow and had a big circular motion and a marvelous follow-through to his forehand. He could hit it either crosscourt or down the line, and he could really whale it. A slugger. I had to see Vines play only once, and from that time on his forehand was my model. I'm not ashamed to admit that I copied his forehand. Every forehand I have hit since first playing with Vines has been with an image of how he hit it.

Kramer: "Ellsworth Vines had a classic forehand . . . and every forehand I ever hit after meeting him was hit with an image of how he did it."

The Case for the Forehand

On the whole, I'd say it's better to be a forehand player than a backhand player. One reason I say this is that the forehand leaves you in a better position after you have hit the shot. Another reason is that, theoretically, you can

hit more shots with the forehand. You can hit the ball harder, and because it's a longer stroke, you can get more speed out of it.

Unfortunately, because the modern game is so quick, many world-class players have what I consider an almost formless forehand. The reason, I think, is that they worry too much about their backhands, often using a forehand grip that leans to the backhand. The result is that they have to pump a lot of wrist into their forehands, and this leads to errors. These errors would not occur, I believe, if more players used the Eastern grip.

Getting Ready

The essence of a good forehand is early preparation. In all cases, when you're in the ready position, I recommend the Eastern forehand grip. Even after you've served or hit a backhand, I recommend returning to that grip. Why? Well, for one thing, the forehand requires a longer swing than the backhand, so you need more time to prepare. Even if you're holding the racquet in the Eastern forehand grip and the ball is hit to your backhand, you have more time to change grips than you would if the situation were reversed.

Not that you shouldn't be ready to change immediately to the backhand. You should. And you can help yourself in this regard by assuming the ready position with the racquet out in front of you and the fingers of the free hand holding the racquet throat lightly, ready to help rotate the racquet in any grip change. Don't cheat by edging over to one side or the other—especially to the backhand side. That will let you in for wasted extra motion in hitting the forehand. Remember, the forehand requires a longer swing anyway. Don't make it harder on yourself.

Another key point in the ready position is flex in your body. You should be in a semi-crouch, your knees slightly bent to help you spring quickly toward the ball. The feet should be spread about shoulder width.

The Swing

Most forehands that go wrong do so right at the start—on the backswing. Beginners usually start their backswing too late. They also don't do enough with it. When the racquet is being drawn back, the hips should be pivoting too, and the proper footwork should be executed at the same time. Most forehand errors can be traced to some breakdown in this preliminary process.

When you're preparing for the forehand, your racquet head should be drawn back so that the face of the racquet is parallel to your body—about at the level of the knee. Concurrently, you should be transferring your weight to your right, or back, foot. In swinging at the ball, you should try to make contact with the ball waist high and carry the stroke through a little higher than the shoulder. When you're stroking the ball, it isn't necessary to flick the wrist, even though some pros do it all the time. Forehands should be hit with a rather firm wrist, as if you were carrying a suitcase. The follow-through (see next section) is crucial. It provides the upward glide to the stroke, thus putting topspin rotation on the ball.

Shifting Weight

Most tennis pros will tell you to shift your weight to the front foot as you hit. And they're right. That's how you do it when you

The topspin forehand in stop action: The racquet, held as flat as possible, should move up from knee level, meet the ball about waist high and then sweep up to shoulder height on the follow-through.

have the time and are ready. But if you are the kind of player who is constantly on the run, you may have to pivot quickly and hit off the back foot. You won't have the time to shift the weight to the front foot.

Given this situation, one might ask why beginners are not taught to hit in this open position, off the back foot. My answer is that a player has to learn the basic steps and body position first and let the variations come with experience. If you're taking piano lessons, you play scales before you play Mozart.

Varying the Stroke

There are essentially three ways to hit a forehand drive: with topspin, in which the ball rises at first, drops sharply and then bounces with a kick; with underspin, in which the ball kind of floats and doesn't bounce as high when it hits, and flat, in which there is no spin at all. Frankly, I think the idea of hitting "flat" is myth. If you're going to hit hard, you have to put spin on the ball in order to control it. And I am a strong advocate of topspin.

Topspin is created by the upward sweep of the racquet to and through the ball. It is a vital element in tennis stroking and should by all means be part of your game. In fact, the two strokes regarded as perhaps the greatest in the history of tennis—Pancho Segura's forehand and Don Budge's backhand—relied heavily on topspin. They applied enough topspin to keep the ball in the court by using a lifting motion of the whole arm and didn't depend on flicking the wrist, the way Rod Laver and Tom Okker do.

Underspin, on the other hand, is created by

a slight backward tilting of the racquet so that the impact of racquet and ball makes the ball spin backward. The ball tends to "float" and has a low bounce when it hits the ground. The great players seldom use underspin on forehand drives from the baseline. It is used primarily for approach shots or as a change of pace to upset the opponent's rhythm.

Rx for Faulty Forehands

Throughout my career, when something went wrong with my forehand—or other parts of my game—I would study movies of myself. It was sometimes hard to believe that the guy on the screen with those flaws was really me. But it's easy to fall into bad habits that cause errors. You may unconsciously develop problems that are impossible for you to detect but easy for others to see.

When a forehand goes bad, it can be for any of several reasons. One is your grip. Faulty preparation and too high a backswing are others. A fourth reason is not swinging soon enough.

Yet another cause of a faulty forehand is not keeping enough flex in the legs while you're running. When you run stiff-legged, you must use too much arm swing to compensate; that reduces your chances of getting off a good shot. Flexing your legs enables you to transfer your weight correctly, which in turn helps promote a smooth, rhythmic stroke.

Summing Up

To summarize, the keys to hitting the power forehand are (1) the proper grip (I recommend the Eastern); (2) early preparation; (3) a swing that starts low and finishes above the shoulder; (4) a firm wrist on contact; (5) a full, smooth follow-through.

The Importance of the Follow-through
by Bill Price

Probably the most common error club players make when hitting the forehand is not following through enough. The racquet is generally stopped shortly after it hits the ball, and the ball, with no spin to guide it, frequently soars up, up and away into the backstop.

There is a simple way to correct this problem. To ensure proper form in the follow-through, you have to bring your arm sufficiently forward after contact so that its upper part forms at least a 90-degree angle with the upper body (see drawing at right). Virtually all good forehand hitters, professionals and juniors alike, get the elbow way forward during the follow-through—toward the direction in which they've hit the ball.

Some players, to put more topspin into their forehands, will finish their forehand stroke with the racquet head well above the head. Other players with good forehands finish with the racquet and racquet handle all the way past the left shoulder. In both cases, the basic rule stays the same: the upper part of the arm must always be raised so that it forms at least a 90-degree angle with the body.

The upper arm in this diagram forms a 90-degree angle with the upper body. Notice too that the elbow is forward. These are two keys that will help you develop the necessary follow-through to a forehand.

The Anatomy of the Power Forehand
by Tony Trabert

When he's on his game, Tom Gorman is one of the strongest all-around performers in tennis. The sequence of photographs here provides a close look at Gorman's forehand. Notice that Gorman uses the circular backswing, as does Jack Kramer. Gorman says this gives him a better sense of rhythm and allows him to hit with more power. My recommendation for average players is that they bring the racquet straight back. This avoids a common error: starting the swing too high. But high backswing notwithstanding, Gorman recovers nicely—getting the racquet down parallel to the ground before contact. And pay special attention to his follow-through. It is excellent.

1. With the ball in play, Tom Gorman is in the ready position awaiting the return. He's about one step behind the baseline and has the racquet pointing straight ahead. That means he'll have the same distance to move it in preparation whether the ball comes to his forehand or his backhand.

2. Realizing that the ball is coming to his forehand, Tom begins his circular backswing as he starts to pivot on the right leg to turn sideways to the net.

3. He continues the backswing while getting sideways with good weight distribution. His feet are wide enough apart now to provide him with good balance.

4. Apparently realizing that the ball is going to land short in his court, Tom slides his right foot forward, which will enable him to stride into the shot with his left foot. The racquet is all the way back, but it is being held quite high in relation to the hitting area.

5. Tom is stepping into the shot, and the racquet is just starting down, in the process of becoming parallel to the ground. This enables him to come in from behind the ball and to hit it with some topspin and power.

6. Because the ball is at his knee level, Tom has bent his knees to get down to the ball, and the racquet is sweeping in behind the area where he plans to contact the ball. His shoulders have started to turn out of the way to permit an unrestricted swing.

7. Gorman has made contact up by his front leg, and the ball is on its way back toward his opponent. Note that Gorman's weight is almost entirely on his forward foot, allowing him to put extra power into the shot.

8. Tom has completed his stroke with a nice high follow-through and a good arm extension. Equally important, notice how he has kept his knees bent throughout the stroke. He did not make the common error of straightening the knees as he hit the ball.

Pancho Segura's Two-handed Forehand
by Ken Bentley

The two-handed forehand of Pancho Segura ranks certainly as one of the most devastating strokes—if not *the* most devastating—in the history of the game. As Jack Kramer puts it: "Of all the forehands I've ever seen, Segura's was the best. The thing Segura had going for him was unpredictability. He could hit it hard when he got set, like a baseball player. But he had ungodly control. He could hit the ball short, crosscourt, long down the line and lob—all with practically the same motion. He had the ability to wait until the last split second, then swing in the direction he wanted to hit the ball."

How did he do it? Here, in the sequence of photographs that follows, Segura demonstrates and explains in his own words.

Swing along with Pancho: Segura tells how he does it. "To use any kind of two-handed shot, you must have good anticipation and fast reflexes in order to get to the ball and to have plenty of time to make the shot. In preparation for the forehand, I wait in an open stance (frames 1 and 2) with my eyes glued to my opponent's racquet so that I can start to move as soon as he hits the ball. I hold my racquet like a baseball bat: my left hand is at the butt of the racquet and the right hand is on top. As my opponent hits the ball, I move laterally with short, rapid steps (frames 3—5) to position myself close to the line of flight of the ball. I start my backswing just about the time the ball hits the ground. The timing is very important, since I prefer to hit the ball at or about waist height. My backswing follows a small circle with my arms quite close to my body (frames 4—8). The two-handed stroke almost forces me to do that. But the small backswing does have the advantage that the shot is easily disguised. As the racquet goes back (frames 5—8), I put my weight entirely on my right foot. That will later force me to bring my body forward so that I can put my weight into the shot. At the end of my backswing (frame 8), the racquet is slightly below the line of flight of the ball, my shoulders are parallel with the line of flight and my knees are bent. On my forward swing (frames 9—11), my racquet remains below the ball and I shift my weight over onto the forward foot. While I'm doing that, I rise slightly off that foot, straightening out my left leg. I meet the ball slightly in front of my body with the racquet face vertical (frame 12). The topspin comes from the movement of the racquet upward as I move it toward and through the ball. At contact, I keep the ball on the strings for as long as possible and follow through out in front (frames 13—15). Then I allow my racquet to finish naturally on my left side (frames 16—18)."

1

2

7

8

13

14

4

5

6

10

11

12

16

17

18

Tom Okker's Lethal Topspin Forehand
by Jack Kramer

Tom Okker, seen in this high-speed photo sequence, has the most unusual forehand in tennis today. It is probably the most potent topspin forehand since Fred Perry's. What makes Okker's forehand all the more amazing is the fact that he does so many things "wrong" with it: he uses a lot of wrist, puts almost no weight into the shot and hits the ball late. Thus it is not a shot the average player should imitate, and yet it is obviously effective. Why? Simply a case of tremendous natural ability overcoming a mechanical and cramped style.

Probably the only orthodox part of Okker's stroke is his ready position (frame 1 on page 36), where he stands with his feet apart, his racquet out in front and his eyes obviously on the ball. But then, as he goes into his looping backswing (3 and 4), he does it with very little arm motion. His wrist is undercocked—that is, he takes his wrist back before his racquet in order to get more zip as he flicks it into the forward swing.

Okker has a very late backswing, since he seems to wait for the ball to bounce before he starts. But that is countered by the speed of the stroke (the elapsed time at the bottom of each frame shows how fast he swings).

As Okker starts his looping forward swing (5 and 6), he transfers his weight to his right foot and maintains a relatively open stance which helps to deceive his opponent about the direction of the shot. His racquet goes well back (6) with a very loose grip and wrist, which will help him whip the racquet around like a piece of spaghetti. As he flicks forward (8), his forehand looks like a Ping-Pong stroke with the racquet going up perpendicularly (9, 10).

In meeting the ball, which he does very late, Okker brings his shoulder around extremely quickly (6 through 11), showing that he does not shift his weight forward for the shot. This shoulder turn, rapid forearm movement and exaggerated wrist snap produce the power in Okker's shot. At impact (10), his wrist begins to close and smother the ball in order to get his topspin action. He hits the ball above the center of his racquet, but it is moving upward so fast that the ball almost rolls off the bottom of the racquet (11). After impact, the racquet continues to rise rapidly (11 through 13) with the force of the wrist snap. Okker has a very complete follow-through (15 and 16), so that he finishes the stroke in a more or less orthodox position.

0.72 seconds 5
0.76 seconds 6
0.82 seconds 7
0.86 seconds 8
0.96 seconds
1.02 seconds
1.12 seconds 15
1.22 seconds 16

The Best Forehands in the Pro Game
by John Alexander

Surprisingly, there are very few top-line players with outstanding forehands. The fact is that the majority of the world's top players, including people like Rod Laver, Ken Rosewall and Jimmy Connors, would rather hit backhand shots.

Who in tennis has the best forehand? To my mind, there are three players whose fore-

Among the players with the top forehands today are John Newcombe (above), Tom Okker (left), Andrés Gimeno (below) and Björn Borg (right), each of whom hits the ball a different way. The leading forehand hitters on the women's circuit are Margaret Court (far right, above) and Kerry Melville Reid (far right, below).

hands deserve special mention: John Newcombe, Andrés Gimeno and Tom Okker. What is interesting about these three is that each hits the forehand in a different way.

Newcombe has a basic, almost classic stroke. He uses a straight backswing, then a slight hesitation, and he comes on to the ball with a slight roll. Newcombe nearly always hits out on his forehand, and he keeps the ball deep, which prevents his opponents from taking the offensive. He passes well, can generate unusual angles hitting crosscourt and is especially dangerous when he's attacking a second serve.

Gimeno's forehand has long been considered one of the best in the game. I don't consider it mechanically as sound as Newcombe's, because he can get a little sloppy on the backswing. But Gimeno always meets the ball right in front of his body, and he always seems to be in good position to hit the stroke. Also, he has a wonderfully long follow-through. I can't think of any player whose racquet seems to follow the flight of the ball as long as Gimeno's. The result is that he hits the forehand with marvelous feel, control, variety and deception—all quite effortlessly. Among the women, Margaret Court's forehand embodies these same elements.

Okker (see analysis on pages 36–37) has one of the most unorthodox forehands in tennis, but certainly one of the most effective. He uses tremendous wrist action, which gives the ball consistently heavy topspin. It's a very difficult shot to contend with, because even if the ball lands short, it will kick up high and long, making a return approach shot very difficult to produce.

Two young players whose heavily topspinning forehands warrant comparison to Okker's are Björn Borg and Guillermo Vilas.

Like Okker, Borg and Vilas rely mainly on a pronounced wrist roll to impart the topspin, but their hitting styles differ in other respects. Vilas' preparation, footwork and weight transfer are more or less in the classic tradition. Because he is quick, he can get into position for shots that other players might have to hit on the run, and he can hit to either side of the court with extraordinary control. Borg, too, has excellent control of his forehand, even though his style is closer to Okker's in its unorthodoxy. Borg uses a Western grip (see page 20) and hits the ball noticeably higher above the net than most players. A ball hit well above the net cannot be hit as hard as a net skimmer, but it is frequently more difficult for an opponent to handle. Borg's forehand invariably lands deep and takes a high lazy bounce, which means that his opponent must supply most of the pace himself in returning it. On clay, where Borg excels and where the rallies are much longer than on other surfaces, returning Borg's forehand time after time can be exhausting. Borg does not hit that many outright winners with his forehand, but his control of the shot, his speed and endurance and the accuracy of his passing shots—which discourages opponents from rushing the net—have the cumulative effect of wearing down his opponents. It is one of the most effective weapons in tennis.

What can the average player learn from these experts? To my mind, the average player would do best to model himself after Newcombe. The key to a dependable forehand is a quick, uncluttered, straight backswing which gives you time to move to the ball and place yourself sideways to the net. It also gives you time to watch the ball to the point of impact and then to follow the flight of the ball with the racquet as far as possible.

Chapter 3 The Backhand

Be Offensive with Your Backhand
by Don Budge

Like most American boys, I played a lot of baseball in my youth. I never achieved great success at the game, but baseball had a lot to do with my success as a tennis player—particularly with my backhand.

The main reason baseball contributed so much to my success in tennis is that while I threw right-handed, I batted left-handed. In other words, what my right, or lead, arm described in the batting swing was essentially a backhand motion. All those hours at home plate paid handsome dividends when I started playing tennis seriously. Hitting the backhand was almost second nature to me.

My baseball experience helped in another way. It gave me two backhand shots: an offensive shot and a defensive shot. Since I had a free and easy tennis swing, it didn't matter whether I was hitting up on the ball to give it topspin, for offensive purposes, or hitting down on the ball to give it underspin, for defensive purposes.

As far as I can tell, most club players today seem to have only one backhand stroke in their repertoire—the defensive shot. This is a shame, because an offensive backhand is not difficult to master. One of the reasons so few club players can hit the backhand offensively is that they are intimidated by the backhand and they hit the backhand defensively, with underspin. Too bad. One of the great joys of tennis is hitting a little roll topspin shot crosscourt—the sort of shot that gives you a great angle and dips below the net level, forc-

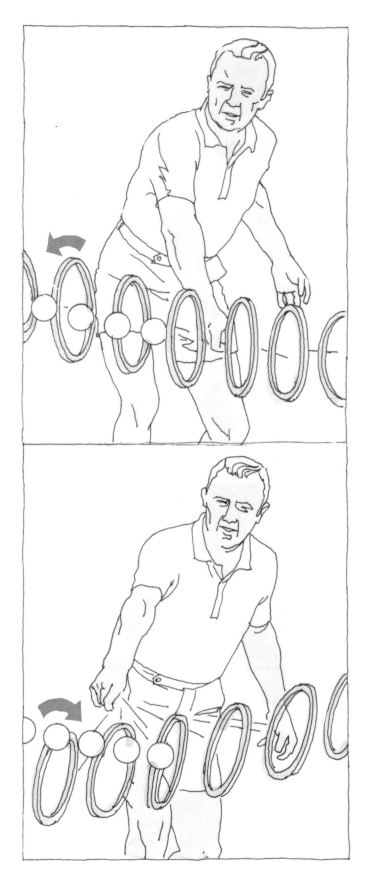

ing your opponent to volley up to you, assuming he can even reach the ball.

The Backhand Fundamentals

Now let's look at the backhand fundamentals. My teaching philosophy has always been to keep things simple. If you want to hit the easy, baseball-style backhand, my advice is to stand sideways, feet spaced comfortably apart, and concentrate on stroking through the ball. Do not *flail* at the ball, like some weak-hitting pitcher trying to hit a Tom Seaver fastball. Relax and use a free and easy stroke. Follow these suggestions and I assure you, the rest of your body—the legs, the shoulders, the arms and the back—will take care of themselves. A good backhand is easier to execute if you don't get in its way.

As for grip, I advise turning the hand about one-eighth turn farther behind the racquet from the Eastern forehand. My grip is exactly the same as the Continental forehand used by such players as Fred Perry, Henri Cochet and Jaroslav Drobný, except that I put my thumb diagonally up behind the back of the handle (see illustration).

Early preparation is crucial. I like to see a player start his backhand stroke by turning sideways, holding his elbow in tight to the body as a good baseball hitter would do. In preparing for the swing, the body should move up on the toes. The elbow should swing easily and naturally. This gives you a sense of uncoiling with power. The follow-through should have no wasted motion; it should feel almost as if you were going to sail the racquet over to your opponent.

One more thing. I recommend bringing the free arm back with the racquet. Since I began as a two-handed hitter, I actually gripped the racquet handle with my left hand. But two-handed or one-handed, the motion is the same. As the racquet goes forward to hit the ball, the free hand should be released and

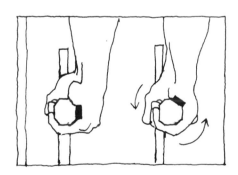

The motion for a right-handed topspin shot resembles the path followed by the right, or lead, arm in a left-handed batting swing. For a proper grip, the flat part of the hand should be placed upon the flat part of the racquet. Then the hand should be rotated about a one-eighth turn farther behind the racquet from its position for the forehand.

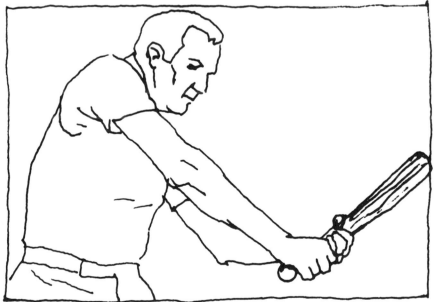

A well-executed backhand starts with the player standing sideways to the approaching ball with his feet placed comfortably apart. If he then strokes through the ball smoothly, the rest of the body—the legs, the shoulders, the arms and the back—will automatically take care of themselves. To hit the offensive shot (right), meet the ball with the racquet on the rise; the result will be a natural, built-in topspin. The follow-through should be a broad, sweeping motion—almost as if the racquet were being sailed over the opposing court.

should fall naturally behind you. A person who has hit a backhand shot correctly should look almost as if he were trying to fly as he goes into the follow-through.

Hitting Offensively

Offensive backhands are hit with topspin. To hit with topspin requires a low backswing and a high finish. The ball is hit with a flat racquet face, but the swinging up imparts enough spin so that the ball can clear the net

by a safe margin and still have the spin to keep it within the baseline.

One way to appreciate the topspin backhand is to compare it to the sort of swing a baseball player makes when he is trying to punch an outside pitch along the ground. He doesn't hit the ball hard, and neither do you to generate topspin. Since you're meeting the ball with a squared-up racquet face, you don't have to worry about turning the racquet face to impart spin. Actually, it's easier to hit a topspin backhand than an underspin backhand.

The Defensive Backhand

Hitting the defensive backhand—that is, one with underspin—involves essentially the same fundamentals as the offensive backhand, with one crucial difference. The racquet is brought back high and you actually swing down on the ball in a "cutting" motion. Obviously, if you swing down, you must make some adjustment to keep the ball from going into the net. That adjustment is a slight upward tilt to the racquet. After the ball is struck, the racquet arcs up slightly from its downward, diagonal path, finishing at about waist level or higher.

Learning the Stroke

Perhaps you think I am oversimplifying the backhand stroke, especially the offensive stroke. Trust me, though. I'm not. Much of the success I achieved in my career I attribute to the topspin in my backhand. But more im-

The defensive backhand, the one most popular with pros and club players alike, is hit with the racquet slicing under the ball at impact and giving it an underspin. Most of the basics in the swing are the same as they are with the offensive shot except that the racquet moves down instead of up. On the follow-through, the racquet swoops down before rising slightly.

portant, where the average player is concerned, I have taken players with very ordinary backhands and by stressing topspin have given a whole new dimension to their game. Sure, the sliced underspin backhand is safer. But give yourself a chance to learn the other way. It can dramatically improve your game.

A Backhand Lesson
by Ken Rosewall

If, like most average players, you'd like to improve your backhand, I can do no better than to stress three points: footwork, hitting the ball early and practice.

Footwork is the key to success in just about every sport. In the tennis backhand, it's a matter of having your feet planted properly as you stroke the ball.

Hitting the ball "early" means hitting the ball on the rise, if you can. A rising ball has more speed than one that's leveling off or sinking. When struck, it will go across the net that much faster.

Finally, practice. You have to work on a backhand so that it becomes almost instinctive. There is no time to think about it in the heat of a match.

At right is a photo sequence taken of me several years ago. In my comments, accompanying the photographs, I have tried to stress the key points that can help you improve your own backhand.

1. Get moving.
Once you see the ball coming to your backhand side, shift your feet around so that they are pointing to the sideline. Skip in short steps, if you have to move for the ball, in order to maintain balance and control. Cradle the throat of your racquet in your nonracquet hand and change to your backhand grip. And be sure to keep your eyes trained on the ball until after you've hit it.

4. Out in front.
As you bring your racquet forward, pivot your waist to turn back toward the net so that your motion will be smooth and controlled. Keep your arm straight and your wrist locked. Just when you're about to hit the ball, shift your weight from your back foot to your front foot. And of course, your knees ought to be bent a bit to allow your weight to move smoothly into the shot. Generally, you should try to hit the ball when it is still slightly in front of you.

2. Be prepared.
You have to allow yourself room to hit the ball with
the arm extended. So as you move, try to judge just
where to pull up to give yourself the room to make
a proper swing. You'll notice that I slice the ball on
this shot—that is, hit the ball with the racquet tilted
slightly back. I do that most of the time because
I feel it gives me greater consistency and control.

3. Elbow room.
Get your feet well planted now, but be ready to
withdraw your front foot a bit if you find yourself too
close to the ball. Turn your shoulders so that your
back is almost facing the net. Keeping a firm wrist,
draw your racquet back fully as early as you can.
Wind it fairly close to your body. And keep your elbow
up and out from the body, remembering that it has
to be held out straight on the forward swing.

5. Take aim.
The moments after impact with the ball are as critical
as those before you've hit it. You must resist the
temptation to lift your head and follow the ball. It must
be watched right onto the racquet (notice my eyes
in this and the preceding photo). At this point, you
should be bringing the racquet around so that it
points toward the spot where you intend the ball to
go. If you're attempting a crosscourt shot, you should
have taken the ball fairly early; a down-the-line shot
must be taken a bit later.

6. Face forward.
On the follow-through, bring your racquet up and
around to a height that's level with your shoulders
or head in order to ensure control of the shot. And
to maintain your balance as well as prepare yourself
for the next shot, turn to face the net. This kind of
follow-through will complete a rhythmical, one-piece
swing—the kind you need for a truly effective
backhand.

The Pros and Cons of the Two-handed Backhand
by Pat McKenna

It works for Chris Evert. It works for Jimmy Connors, Björn Borg and Billy Martin. And it works for Cliff Drysdale. But what about the two-handed backhand for the average player? Most pros advise against it, but perhaps it is time for a reevaluation.

Comparing the Strokes

In order to evaluate the two-handed backhand, it is useful to consider how it differs from the one-handed backhand.

In the two-handed backhand, the racquet is generally held with both hands in the Eastern forehand grip. If you are right-handed, your right hand will be closer to the bottom of the grip and your left hand will be right above it. (It's the other way around for left-handers.) The backswing is closer to the body and a little lower than it is in the typical one-handed backhand. The forward swing is upward, as if you were hitting for topspin one-handed, and both elbows bend just after contact, with the follow-through continuing upward and over the right shoulder. The swing is not quite as long as in the one-handed backhand, but the footwork and positioning of the feet are pretty much the same.

Advantages of the Two-handed Backhand

Make no mistake about it, there are definite advantages to the two-handed backhand. Among them:

1. It's an easier stroke to teach to young children and players who are not strong enough to handle the one-handed backhand.
2. It's easier to generate topspin with the stroke.
3. It's a little easier to hit the ball with power.
4. It's easily grooved and has a tendency to stay grooved.
5. It is particularly good for players who have equal dominance with both hands.

Chief among present-day practitioners of the two-handed backhand are Chris Evert (above left), whose success with the two-handed shot is keyed to her keen sense of anticipation and well-disciplined footwork; Jimmy Connors (above right), who hits nearly everything hard and flat; Björn Borg (left), who generates considerable topspin with the stroke; and Cliff Drysdale (below), whose two-handed shot is always hit with force and consistency.

Weaknesses of the Two-handed Backhand

The weaknesses of the two-handed backhand are as follows:

1. It cuts down on reach.
2. It makes hitting high and low balls more difficult.
3. It must be hit with precise footwork and a solid stance.
4. It is a difficult stroke to slice.
5. It is sometimes difficult to hit a return of serve that cramps the backhand side.
6. It breeds a tendency to slap at shots.
7. It may give a 10-year-old a "crutch" that will be hard to discard at 16 years of age when he or she is bigger and stronger.

Considering the Alternative

The alternative to the two-handed backhand, of course, is the traditional one-handed backhand. It, too, has relative weaknesses. It requires a change of grip, if you use the Eastern grips. It's a difficult shot for young children to learn. It is more difficult to groove and, when hit late, it doesn't afford the power that the two-handed stroke does.

On the other hand, the one-handed backhand has the following virtues:

1. It permits greater reach.
2. It allows for greater flexibility in hitting a range of different shots.
3. It doesn't require the footwork precision needed on the two-handed and can be hit more effectively off balance.
4. Its longer follow-through makes it easier to hit deeper shots without an excessively fast swing.
5. It's a smoother stroke.
6. It makes hitting low and high balls a little easier.

The Verdict

When weighing the effectiveness (or lack of it) of the two-handed backhand, it seems to me that physical strength is the most important consideration. My own feeling is that only weaker and smaller players should develop the two-handed backhand, and I don't include here the young player who has the potential of adequate strength and size.

But if you still feel, for any reason, that the two-handed backhand is better for you, then, by all means, pursue the stroke with enthusiasm and confidence. At the same time, be aware of the inherent weaknesses of the stroke and develop the skills to counteract them. The two-handed player needs to work hard on footwork, speed and anticipation if he is to be successful.

Chris Evert's Two-handed Backhand
by Alice Marble

The best backhand among current women players, in my opinion, belongs to Chris Evert. It is, of course, a two-handed stroke, and she uses it with devastating effect.

Because so few major players have been successful with it, I have never been a strong advocate of the two-handed shot. The power is there, but a player has to move much more quickly to get to the ball, since using two hands requires that the stroke be hit close to the body. Still, you can't argue with Chris's success. In the stop-action photo sequence, let's examine the perfect form of the Evert two-handed backhand.

1. Step out.
Right from the start of the stroke, Chris is in perfect position, with her racquet back. She's stepping out with the right foot—a must for a good backhand—and her weight is perfectly balanced on the balls of her feet. Note that her eyes are carefully following the ball.

2. Turn sideways.
She is now switching her balance to her left foot. Her body is starting to assume the proper sideways position. That will ensure getting enough backswing for the power that is needed. At this point, her knees are slightly flexed.

3. Watch the ball.

Chris concentrates hard as she looks over her right shoulder at the oncoming ball. Her weight stays on her left foot. The racquet is still back in a high position. Her right foot is starting to point to the sideline.

4. Racquet down.

Now Chris's racquet is starting to drop to a lower position to enable her to impart topspin to the ball. Her right foot is about to step sideways and forward. You can see that she almost has her back to the net —which is essential to ensure enough backswing.

5. Up to the ball.

This picture is perhaps the most telling of all. The racquet is coming up to the ball to give it that topspin. Chris is swinging out to catch the ball about waist high—the ideal spot in which to meet the ball. Her right foot is pointing perfectly to the sideline.

6. At arm's length.

As Chris meets the ball, her eyes are carefully focused. She is hitting the ball quite far from her body and is using the full length of both arms to get power. Now her weight is on the right foot.

7. Over the ball.

Much like that of a top golfer, Chris's head is down after the ball is hit. Her body is in perfect balance. The racquet is coming slightly over the ball, imparting the topspin. But the ball is stroked high enough for it to clear the net.

8. Follow-through.

Chris's follow-through is high and her head is still. However, the position of her feet is not perfect. Those crossed legs do not ensure good balance. But that is a Chris Evert characteristic that doesn't seem to impair her otherwise perfect shot.

The Best Backhands
in the Pro Game
by John Alexander

There are so many good backhands in tennis today, it's difficult to single out the few that stand out above the rest; but certainly three of the very best belong to Rod Laver, Ken Rosewall and Arthur Ashe. Interestingly enough, as we saw earlier with top forehand players (page 38), the styles of the three are noticeably different. Laver does not have classic form—he doesn't take much of a backswing—but he times the stroke very well and snaps his powerful wrist to give the ball a great deal of topspin. He is especially dangerous with the shot on return of service. Rosewall's backhand, of course, is considered by most people to be almost as good as Don Budge's. He has a rather high backswing and hits the ball with a slight amount of underspin. The key to Rosewall's success is footwork. He never hits off balance. What makes Rosewall so tough is that he can do so much with his backhand. He can go down the line with it or crosscourt, and he has the ability to mix in a soft dink and a variety of lobs, all with great deception. Ashe has a freewheeling, wristy backhand that he hits with tremendous power. Because he can delay on the shot more than most players, he can wait until his opponents commit themselves before he hits it.

Another backhand that certainly deserves mention is Cliff Drysdale's. Drysdale, of course, hits his backhand two-handed; like Rosewall, he can go down the line or crosscourt with equal power, but he's not as versatile with it.

As different as these fine backhands are, they share certain similarities from which the average player can learn: early backswing, concentration on the ball and a follow-through along the intended flight of the ball. These are the fundamentals of all good backhands. Keep the stroke easy. When you take the racquet back, your shoulders should face the side of the court and your right foot, crossing over, should make a firm foundation for the stroke. Practicing the fundamentals described above will put you well on the way to developing an improved backhand game.

The pro ranks are loaded with players with outstanding backhands, chief among them Evonne Goolagong Cawley (left), Ken Rosewall (above), Arthur Ashe (below), and Rod Laver (right).

Chapter 4 The Volley

The Forehand Volley
by Dennis Ralston

The volley is obviously a vital part of modern tennis—a shot that every player with any aspirations toward developing a sound, all-around game must attempt to master. But why be grim about it? Volleys are fun.

The Basics

In hitting the forehand volley, two factors are of paramount importance. The first is hitting the ball in front of you. The second is letting the racquet do most of the work. Too many players try to muscle the ball on a volley by taking a full arm swing. It's not necessary. By keeping the racquet as extended as circumstances demand and by letting the wrist provide part of the power for the swing, you can generate all the speed, strength and control you need.

When to Volley

When and how often you volley in a match will depend a great deal on how skillful a volleyer you are, how aggressive a game you like to play and the sort of game your opponent plays. In doubles you don't have too much choice, but in singles the choice is pretty much up to you.

The volley stroke itself dictates pretty much the circumstances under which it should be hit. To be effective, a volley should be hit in front of the service line (toward the net). But to hit the volley you have to be there when the ball is there. So to volley effectively, you must first be quick enough to assume a strong position at the net and, secondly, be able to hit approach shots that put your opponent under enough pressure so that he can't lob or pass you to death. Some teaching professionals advise against coming to the net on slow surfaces, but since my own game is an attacking one I look for a chance to volley even on very slow courts. True, I sometimes have to wait awhile for the right time, but eventually I come in.

The Volleying Position

Position is crucial in hitting volleys. To my mind, the ideal position for volleying in singles is a foot or two in front of the service line, and straddling the center line. In this position, you can protect yourself from passing shots on either side, plus you can protect

Dennis Ralston demonstrates here and on the next page the keys to the forehand volley.

The photographs illustrate the fundamentals of successful volleying. Notice that in frame 1 he is facing the net, knees bent, with his free hand cradling the racquet at the throat. In photo 2 notice the short backswing and the position of the wrist, which is bent slightly. The racquet head is slightly open. In photo 3 Ralston attacks the ball with the wrist still bent, but with the racquet head snapping forward. The wrist, however, is firm on contact with the ball. The follow-through shown in photo 4 is short and compact.

yourself from the lob. One of the most common errors club players make is to stand too close to the net when hitting volleys. I grant you that you can get some tough angles on volleys hit there, but you are extremely vulnerable to the lob.

Getting Set

I recommend the Continental grip (page 19) for all volleys. The main reason for this is that net play involves split-second timing. You simply don't have enough time to change grips. The Continental grip is a halfway measure. It allows you to hit backhand or forehand volleys without changing grips.

In getting ready to hit the forehand volley, position yourself with your feet comfortably apart and pointing to the net. The knees should be slightly bent—almost, not quite, in a boxer's crouch—and the throat of the racquet should be cradled lightly in the free hand. Not only does the free hand help to support the racquet; it can push the racquet head off toward the direction the ball is coming from. And don't forget that the racquet head—not the arm—must do the moving.

Footwork: Less Is More

One widespread bit of advice about the forehand volley is that you should always "step, swing and hit." Pros who advocate this approach maintain that your other leg—the one opposite the stroking side—should be crossed in front of the body toward the ball. Well, I don't think this is very good advice. The problem is that if you take the time to cross that leg over, you increase the chances of meeting the ball behind you.

When you get into the proper position to hit the ball, the weight should be back on the foot on the stroking side, with that foot remaining still pointing. The other foot should be moved directly forward and placed at an angle approximately 45 degrees to the net. Your weight shifts, but your feet don't.

The Swing

The volley swing is short and compact: a quick slap. On the backswing, the wrist should be broken slightly. The racquet should be brought back no farther than the shoulder. At this point, the racquet head can be slightly open (tilted a bit backward). But as the racquet comes forward, the racquet head should be returned to the straight-up position so that the shot is hit fairly flat. The wrist, meanwhile, remains bent as the racquet is snapped forward but should be firm at the moment of contact. The point of contact should be well out in front of the body. Ideally, at the moment of contact on a forehand volley, the racquet of a right-handed player should be stuck out at approximately a 2-o'clock angle. Your follow-through is very short—the racquet should not go beyond the ready position. Go any further and you compromise your ability to get the racquet back to the ready position, and in the rat-a-tat-tat of net play you can't afford to waste time.

It is particularly important to keep your eye on the ball when volleying. This isn't too hard, because on the volley there is always the impulse to focus on the ball when it is hit near you. Another thing: You don't have to kill the ball—particularly on an easy shot. At the net, more points are won with placement than with power. Don't try for fantastic shots.

If you do manage to pull one off, don't stand there admiring it; your opponent is not likely to share your delight, and there's always the chance he will return it.

Moving Side to Side

The forehand volley would be a simple shot if your opponent always obliged you by hitting where you happen to be standing, but tennis doesn't work that way. One way to contend with a volleyer is to pass him. This means you will do some stretching. If a passing shot comes to your forehand side, the basic stroking principles are the same. The main thing is to get the racquet head out first. That cuts down on the amount of time needed to get to the ball. You break your wrist slightly, slapping at the ball and hitting it out in front of you, hopefully, at that 2-o'clock angle.

Even more difficult than the passing shot is the drive hit right at you. If the drive has been hit to you from the forehand side of the net, you will volley with your forehand. Here footwork is important. You should step back with your right foot (left, if you are left-handed) and at the same time pull your right shoulder back. This position will allow you to hit the volley with the normal stroke. If the ball is on top of you too quickly, just try to block it—making sure the racquet head is out in front of you.

Summing Up

Most of the problems that arise with the forehand volley—even among tournament players—can be traced to a problem with one of the two fundamentals mentioned above: hitting the ball out in front and letting the racquet do most of the work. There are no great secrets to hitting winning volleys. Keep the stroke simple and compact. Shorten your backswing and cut down your follow-through. You may be surprised at how easy it can be.

How I Hit the Backhand Volley
by Tony Trabert

The backhand volley played a pivotal role in getting my tennis career started. As a pudgy young kid of 12, I was practicing backhand volleys one summer morning in 1942 at the Cincinnati Tennis Club, where the Tri-State Tennis Championships were being contested. Bill Talbert, then one of the top-ranked players in the nation, happened by and noticed me. He paused to give me a few pointers about the stroke, mainly advising me to keep the racquet out in front and to punch at the ball.

The next morning I was out there again practicing, and again Talbert stopped by with some advice. The same thing happened on the third day. I guess he felt I had some potential as a player and could see I was willing to work at the game. So he took me under his wing and through the years became the most influential force in my development as a player. I've always been grateful for his help and encouragement—and it all started with those backhand volleys years ago in Cincinnati.

The Grip

For the backhand volley I recommend the Eastern backhand grip (see page 18). This is not the grip the pros use. Most pros use the Continental grip for all volleys, since the quick exchanges at the net make changing grips impractical. But in the beginning I think it's smart to start with the basic backhand grip and then switch once you've mastered other elements of the stroke.

Preparing for the Stroke

In the ready position for the backhand volley, the feet should be spread a little more than shoulder width apart. The knees should be slightly bent and you should be in a slight crouch. Your weight should be forward, on the balls of your feet. This will enable you to make a quick start in whatever direction proves necessary. The racquet head should be above the hand holding the racquet, and the racquet should be directly in front of you.

A Volley Tip

Here's a little tip that can go a long way in helping you hit a better backhand volley.

1. To prepare for the backhand volley, stand in the ready position with the feet spread apart and with the arms extended comfortably so that contact with the ball can be made well out in front of the body.

2. As the ball comes up, the racquet should be pulled back, the knees bent and the weight shifted forward on the balls of the feet. Keeping the weight forward will allow for a quick step toward the ball, if necessary.

3. In volleying, there's no time for a full backswing. So the racquet should be brought back, with the hand holding the throat, only as far as the shoulder. At the same time, a step can be made into the ball.

4. Contact with the ball should be made in a short punching motion. The whole movement of the racquet now should be down and forward; it should be tilted back so that it gives the ball enough underspin to clear the net.

5. A good volley demands that the wrist be kept firm and the arm straight. The ball must be hit well in front of the body so that the ball can be seen at all times. Stepping forward helps put weight behind the stroke.

6. The follow-through for the backhand volley is, of necessity, abbreviated. Almost as soon as contact is made with the ball, the racquet should be stopped so that it's ready for a fast return.

When you're in the ready position at the net, make sure your arms are extended comfortably forward and that your *elbows are in front of your body*. With elbows in front, you'll be able to hit the volley well in front of your body and that way be able to see the ball at all times. If you wait with your elbows by your side, as most players do, your racquet will still be at your side when you react to a quick return, and you'll never get a chance to see the ball.

Executing the Backhand Volley

Backhand volleys are best hit with a short, chopping motion. As the ball approaches, the free hand should pull the racquet back, but not too far. If you have the time, you should turn to the side so that you can step off with your front foot as you punch the volley. Some pros may tell you not to worry much about footwork in the volley, but I think it's important.

Wrist action is also important (see page 65). As you prepare to hit the ball, your wrist should be cocked. It snaps forward as you make your swing but remains firm at the moment of contact. A well-executed volley is actually a sharp forward push, the racquet head and wrist moving forward in unison. Whatever you do, do not flick the racquet head at the ball. Use your forearm and wrist, hitting down and forward on the ball. This creates the underspin that will keep the ball in the court. Also, the ball should be hit as far out in front of the body as possible. There should be little or no follow-through, because you want the racquet to remain in the hitting area in the event the ball comes back quickly, which it often does in doubles.

Low Volleys

On low volleys, the face of the racquet should be tilted back slightly and the shot should be executed with a short punch forward. The racquet face has to be tilted back to enable the ball to come up quickly so that it can clear the net. Low volleys are difficult because you have to get the ball up and over the net and still keep it in the court. My advice on low volleys is to recognize that you are in trouble, watch the ball closely, make a short punch at the ball and strive to hit it deep into your opponent's court—but not too hard. If you try to hit the low volley too hard, you'll either catch the tape or hit it past the baseline.

High Volleys

On the high backhand volley, you do best to make contact in front of your body, so that you can see the ball at all times, and try to punch the ball deep. This is a difficult shot for most players, so don't try to be a hero. Get it back deep and prepare for the next volley. Don't always try to hit a winner off your first volley. Sometimes it takes a couple of volleys before you get your opponent out of position, at which point you can more easily win the point with the third volley.

It is best to step forward with your front foot as you make your backhand volley in order to get some body weight into the shot. If you don't have time to take that step, at least be sure to keep the racquet out in front of you and punch the ball. Or in extreme circumstances, simply try to block it back.

Direct Shots

How should you handle a ball coming straight toward you at the net? Since everything is moving so fast, it has to be basically a reflex action. But if you have the time to choose between a forehand and a backhand volley, go with the one you feel is your strong shot. It's strictly personal preference.

In the case of the backhand volley, I get my racquet parallel to the net immediately, and at the same time, I step directly sideways to my right (since I'm right-handed) with my right foot. As I make this move, my knees are bent in the suggested ready position. This permits me to transfer all the weight over to my right leg. I can then make contact with the ball not when it's out in front of me, but when it's to the left side of my body. By stepping to the side, I get my body out of the way and am in a position to make a good volley off a potentially difficult shot.

On low backhand volleys, most good volleyers go for depth to stay out of trouble, often sacrificing pace for safety. But on all volleys higher than the net, the best players are very aggressive. They try to win the point outright off the high volley. Forget the cute angles and drop volleys; they are low-percentage shots, and you'll lose many more points than you'll win with them. Let the pros execute those toughies.

Rx for Backhand Volleys

If you are having trouble with your backhand volley, perhaps this checklist will help you.

1. Watch the ball like a hawk.
2. Use a backhand grip.
3. Have your free hand on the throat of the racquet.
4. Keep your wrist firm.
5. Tilt the face of the racquet back slightly and use a chopping motion that moves from high to low.
6. Take a short jab at the ball with little or no backswing and no follow-through.
7. Make contact as far out in front of the body as possible.

Wrist Action on the Volley
by Chet Murphy

Tennis instructors are always alert for colorful words and simple techniques that help make their teaching effective. Among the most common are "block" and "punch"—two words frequently used to describe the volley motion. These terms are descriptive to a point, but neither conveys the crucial action of the wrist in the skilled volley shot.

A better approximation of the volley is found in the childhood game of patty-cake. Hold a racquet in your hand and play "patty-cake" with an imaginary figure for a while and you will begin to approximate the correct wrist action for the volley.

In this photo series of the talented woman pro Julie Anthony (below), photographs 2 and 3 show the "patty-cake" action in volley.

Notice the ready position in photo 1 and the cocked and laid-back wrist in photos 2 and 3. By maintaining this wrist position throughout the entire stroke, the player retains control of the racquet and avoids the loose swing that usually results in inaccurate hitting.

What force the player does need is attained by stepping into the shot and by extending the forearm as shown in photo 4.

Hitting the High
Backhand Volley
by Bill Murphy

The high backhand volley is one of the most difficult shots in tennis. It is particularly difficult for most players to hit with power. In its mechanics, the stroke is actually similar to that of a backhand volley hit waist high, except that you must hit *down* on the ball. The motion should be crisp, with the elbow straightening as the ball is met slightly forward of the body. If you have the time, it is best to hit this stroke with both feet facing the sideline. As the photograph below indicates, the wrist is very firm on this stroke. The wrist angle should remain rather constant throughout the stroke. In other words, you should not try to "wrist" backhand volleys. The forearm executes the stroke, although your weight should be moving forward as you hit it. As with all volleys, the follow-through is very short.

The key to success in hitting the high backhand volley as pro Phil Dent shows is to keep a very firm wrist, straighten the elbow at impact and follow through short.

How to Hit the Half Volley
by Roy Emerson

The half volley is a stroke you are forced to use when a ball is aimed at your feet or when you can't rush the net fast enough to volley the ball before it bounces. It is a shot taken almost immediately after the ball bounces, at just about ground level. It is not a shot you go out of your way to hit. The occasion for hitting it arises frequently in doubles when the ball is hit right at your feet, or in singles when you're following in your serve and your opponent hits a well-paced drive that's going to bounce before you can volley it back. You could, of course, retreat in this situation and hit the shot as a normal ground stroke, but that would keep you away from the net. Besides, when you have to change direction abruptly like that it is difficult to recover your balance, and the result is usually a weak backhand or forehand.

Getting Down

The most important thing to remember about the half volley is that you should get down on the ball as much as possible, even if it means actually touching the ground with your knees. The ball should be hit slightly in front of you with an upward motion and as full a follow-through as you can generate from your knees-bent position. Your weight should be moving forward. You don't need an extended follow-through—just enough of one to help you achieve the direction in which you want the ball to go.

Also crucial to this stroke is the angle of the racquet face. From your short backswing, the racquet should be brought forward, with the racquet head up as much as possible and with the face slightly open (tilted back). The closer you are to the net, the more you'll have to open the racquet face to make sure the ball clears the net. Open the face too much, however, and you'll end up lifting the ball over the net for a weak lob. Practice should help you judge the proper racquet angle.

Learning from the Master

I guess the true expert at the half volley is Ken Rosewall. Rosewall has to hit a lot of half volleys because his opponents are always slamming balls at his feet. The key to his success with the stroke is his marvelous footwork and good balance. He is able to get very low on the ball without losing his balance, and he hits with such a fluid, economical motion that he resembles a slick-fielding shortstop picking up a ground ball. Those are the keys, really: getting to the ball, getting down on it, hitting with a fluid motion—and, of course, keeping an eye on the ball. On the following pages, I demonstrate how it's done.

Most half volleys are hit when you are on your way to the net and don't have time to get close enough to the ball to volley it before it bounces (frame 1). As soon as you realize that the situation calls for a half volley, stop (2), pivot to get your shoulders around parallel to the flight of the ball and step toward the ball with your front foot (3). Get down as low as possible (4, 5), but keep your racquet head up as much as possible (6). You'll need only a short backswing (5, 6), but you'll be able to get

enough power into the shot by keeping your body weight forward (7). At contact (8),
keep a firm wrist and forearm and hit the ball with the racquet face slightly open (9).
Carry the ball on your racquet for as long as possible, and try for as much follow-
through as you can manage from your bending position (10, 11, 12). Follow through
in the direction in which you are aiming the ball.

The Best Volleys in the Pro Game

by John Alexander

The first player who really impressed me with his volleying was Frank Sedgman, the great Australian champion of the early 1950's. Sedgman's volley—forehand or backhand—was a marvelous shot, played strictly with a punching action and hit as far out in front as he could comfortably reach. What really made it effective was his quickness in leaping forward to take the volley as close to the net as possible.

Lew Hoad, who came along a few years later, also had a much-feared volley. In fact, it was feared by no less a player than Richard ("Pancho") Gonzalez. In their first head-to-head showdown involving a series of 100 matches, Gonzalez completely rebuilt his backhand (which previously he had much preferred to hit down the line) so that he could play it offensively crosscourt and thereby avoid the Hoad forehand volley.

As Gonzalez said, "I was getting killed by Lew simply because my best shot was my backhand down the line and Lew's was his forehand volley. It meant that he would thump crosscourt in such a fashion I would be unable even to get my racquet on the ball."

There are a couple of fellows around now who also possess very formidable forehand volleys. John Newcombe has a drive volley (a volley that is hit as if it were a ground stroke) that is the best among contemporary players. He plays it from midcourt, often off a lofted return of serve. He employs only a slightly shorter swing than he does with a normal high forehand and seems to use less body ac-

tion. His normal forehand volley, much admired, is played with the head of the racquet well up and with a very firm wrist. Dennis Ralston also has a superior forehand volley. His great strength is that he strictly observes basic principles, uses very little backswing, follows through with the head of the racquet held up firmly and keeps his eyes on the ball.

Of the outstanding backhand volleys, I'd have to rate Arthur Ashe's as one of the best in the game. The key to Ashe's effectiveness on this stroke is that he meets the ball well in front of his body. This is not easy to do, but the value of it is that it enables you to keep the ball in view and to hit the ball at a time when it's easiest to coordinate eye and hand—that is, when the ball is approaching on a line and not when it's on top of you or streaking past. Ashe never loses sight of the ball and, as a result, can make deadly accurate placements.

Bob Lutz, Erik Van Dillen and Ken Rosewall are three other players whose backhand volleys are effective. The beauty of Rosewall's is that you never know where he's going to place it. That's how well he disguises the stroke. Van Dillen's is deceptive too, and he gives the shot added character by putting heavy underspin on the stroke through a sharp slicing motion. Lutz doesn't disguise his backhand as well as Rosewall or Van Dillen, but he makes up for this by generating an incredible amount of angle. He does this by using a very sharply cocked wrist when he strikes the ball—a technique I do not recom-

The best forehand volleyers of recent years have included these three champions: Frank Sedgman (left), John Newcombe (above), and Lew Hoad (below).

Among the world's best backhand volleyers are Billie Jean King (left), Arthur Ashe (above) and Evonne Goolagong Cawley (below). Billie Jean's ability to hit behind opponents going the opposite way makes her backhand volley one of the best offensive weapons in tennis.

mend for the average player because it's difficult to keep the cocked wrist firm on a hard-hit ball.

And let's not forget Roy Emerson. Emerson has an unorthodox lunging action that looks awkward but is extremely effective. Emmo can hit winners no matter what direction the ball is coming from, and the key, in his case, is good concentration, aggressiveness and a lot of forward weight into the shot.

Not many of the women pros seem to have effective volleys. Evonne Goolagong Cawley has perhaps the best, even though her movements are a little sloppy. What she does very well is meet the ball well in front, rather like Ashe. Billie Jean King's backhand volley is effective too. It was her ability to place it in either corner that helped her destroy Bobby Riggs in their famous match. She doesn't hit it hard, but she places it well and isn't afraid of the shot.

Developing an effective backhand volley—or a forehand volley—is largely a matter of a lot of practice at the net. In summing up, I can do no more than reiterate the advice given by Dennis Ralston in the first section of this chapter. Hit the ball in front of you, let the racquet do most of the work and, above all, keep your eye on the ball at all times.

Chapter 5 The Serve

Getting More Firepower into the Cannonball
by Arthur Ashe

Arthur Ashe demonstrates the powerful cannonball serve.

The serve is, by all odds, the single most important stroke in modern tennis. Think about it. It's the only shot you hit that is not a return of a shot by your opponent. As you stand at the baseline, you and you alone are in control of the point. Generally speaking, the point will be decided on how well you put the ball into play.

I have built my game around the serve and the backhand. When things are going well, the serve can win the point for me, or at least set things up so that it will be over after two volleys.

There are three basic types of serves: the flat, which I'll describe and demonstrate for you here; the slice and the American twist, both of which will be described in subsequent sections.

The flat serve—or cannonball, as it's also called—is the most spectacular serve of the three. When it is properly executed, the ball is struck in the middle of the racquet, with the racquet face square and hence with little or no spin on the ball. When it's hit well, no other serve comes across the net as fast.

And that's the problem. Too many players on ego trips use the flat serve simply to prove how overpowering they can be. They fire away indiscriminately in an attempt to chalk up aces—never mind that they sacrifice points in the form of double faults in the process. We will return to this problem later. Now let's consider the fundamentals of the serve.

The Starting Position

The right way to begin the flat serve—or any serve, for that matter—is to stand relaxed with your weight on the front foot and both hands held close together at waist level.

In singles, the place to stand is right up against the center mark. This position represents the shortest distance between you and the other service court. In doubles, where control of the net is your goal, the place to stand is about midway between the center mark and the singles sideline. This positions you for the shortest possible route to your proper place at the net.

In positioning yourself, stand so that your belly is facing the net post on your right (for right-handers, that is). The feet should be about shoulder width apart, with the right foot nearly parallel to the baseline. I generally start my serve with my left foot 12 inches or so behind the baseline and then I move it up as I swing. This is a quirk I developed as a youngster, and I don't recommend it. In fact, the USLTA had to hold special deliberations a few years ago to determine that the little step of mine was legal.

Let It Flow

When you begin your serving motion, you should be loose and relaxed. Your aim is to make your service one long, free rhythmic motion. Once the action starts, it isn't necessary to muscle your way through it. Let the motion take care of itself. Let the racquet flow through the ball. The motion should be as smooth as possible, with no hitches.

It's not that easy, I realize. Service action involves the coordination of two separate movements: getting the ball up and bringing the racquet around. Ideally, the racquet should meet the ball at the top of the swing. The key here is the ball toss. It is best on the flat serve to throw the ball a bit higher than the projected contact point so that you can hit the ball just as it is beginning its descent. This requires extensive practice, but you have to do it if you want to hit the flat serve with any consistency. Hold the ball with the pads at the ends of the thumb and the first three fingers. Hold only one ball at a time. It is inadvisable to hold two on a first serve for two reasons. First, if the serve goes in, either you have to play the point carrying a ball in your hand or else you have to remember to throw it aside. Why do that? Second, with another ball in your hand if you miss the first serve, you're inclined to rush the second serve instead of taking your time as you should. So put the second ball in your pocket. (If your tennis dress doesn't have a pocket, ladies, sew one on.)

Rocking in Rhythm

Some players, myself included, like to serve with a kind of rocking motion. It helps establish a rhythm for the stroke. It's like winding up and then letting go. After beginning with both hands at waist height and with the weight on my left foot, I rock my weight back onto my right foot and drop both arms so that the elbows are straight. Then I begin to move the left arm upward and the right arm into the backswing. It is vital to rhythm and coordination that both arms move into action at the same time. It also simplifies things.

The Swing

As your left arm tosses the ball, your right arm should begin taking the racquet back in as big an arc as possible; keeping your elbow up and out as far from your body as you can will help achieve this. The closer the elbow is to the body, the smaller the arc. You want a big arc, to give you as much leverage on the serve as you can get. With a big arc, your arm will be fully extended upon contact with the ball, and this ensures maximum power.

Bring the racquet around behind you as quickly and comfortably as you can; the farther you bring it down behind you, the harder you are likely to hit the ball. Once the racquet is behind you, bend your knees, arch your back and shift your weight back onto your right foot. At this point your shoulders should be perpendicular to the net and your body should be coiled like a rubber band.

Now that you're coiled this way, you unwind yourself by moving your right leg forward. It's this motion which gives speed to your flat serve. But there are others, too. The torque of your body as it winds up and then releases is one. So is the timing of the whole motion, which requires lots of practice to perfect.

Wrist Action in the Cannonball

Wrist action is important in all types of serves, but especially in the cannonball, where your main purpose is to generate power. During the backswing, the wrist should be held in its natural, uncocked position. But once it swings over your head and behind your back, it should be cocked. This will drop the racquet even farther behind your back. At contact, the wrist should snap forward from its cocked position. This snapping of the wrist is the final energy source of a process that derives its overall power from a combination of body weight, arm movement and the whipping action of the racquet head.

After the ball has been struck, your body should be leaning well into the court and be stretched out in almost a straight line from your fingers to your ankles. I don't mean ramrod straight, but relatively straight. After my serve, I am far enough out over the court at contact that if I dropped my racquet it would land almost three feet inside the baseline.

At contact, your shoulders should be parallel to the net, with the left hand tucked in close to the body to help maintain balance against the force of the racquet arm hurling forward. Then the racquet should be brought down across the body and around to the left side in a smooth, complete follow-through.

Also, when you finish the serve, you should have made an almost 180-degree turn with your belly button practically facing the net post on your *left*. You should be peering over your right shoulder as you head toward the net. If you don't want to rush the net, your right foot should serve as the brace against which you bounce back to the sideline.

Conclusions

As effective as the cannonball serve can be, I don't think you should rely on it unless you can get it in about 65 percent of the time on your first serve. I strongly advise against using the flat serve on the second serve. The margin of error is too great. Since the ball is on a flat trajectory, it must clear the net by a

As I start to serve, I stand with my hands close together at about waist level and my weight on my forward foot (1). Then I swing my weight back and drop both arms so that my elbows are straight (2). My left arm then begins to go upward for the ball toss (3) and my right arm continues taking my racquet back in a large arc (5—7) until it reaches the position where I can cock my arm to put the racquet into a "back-scratching" position (8—9). At the same time, I release the ball around shoulder level (4) but with a kind of short follow-through (5) that helps me to position the ball

accurately. When the ball is in the air I bend my knees, arch my back and shift my weight onto my left foot (5—7). Then I unwind by moving forward and stretching upward (8—10). For a flat serve, I hit the ball when it's to my right and out in front of me (11). Now my shoulders are parallel to the net and my left arm is tucked into my body (12). Next, I bring my racquet down across my body (13) and follow through around to my left side (14). From this position, I can either rush the net or brace myself to stay back on the baseline.

few inches at most or else it will land out of the service court. It is more advisable to use a slice or twist on the second serve, as most of the pros do. If you follow the basics I've outlined, and if you work on them, you should be able to develop an effective flat serve. It is not an easy serve to master, and there are days when it will fail you. But when it's working, it can be a devastating weapon—and lots of fun to hit, too.

The Slice Serve
by Tony Trabert

As Arthur Ashe pointed out in the last article, even accomplished players do not rely solely on a flat service. They depend on the slice serve. The value of a slice serve is twofold: First, it arrives in the receiver's court with a little more speed than the typical "patsy" serve most club players use on a second serve, and it also has a deceptive bounce. Secondly, it is easier to control than the flat serve.

Basically, the slice serve has sidespin. It will bounce away from a right-handed opponent's forehand, or can be served into the left side of his body to cramp him on his return. If your opponent is in the deuce court, for example, you can serve near the singles sideline, run him out of court to retrieve the shot and set yourself up for a winner on his return.

The accompanying sequence photographs spell out in detail how to hit a slice serve. The basics of the stroke are as follows: Use a backhand grip, toss the ball slightly to the right of the body and forward of the baseline, and swing toward the right net post, with the racquet going around the side of the ball on contact. The follow-through finishes on the left side of your body. If the slice is well hit, it will curve from the receiver's left to his right. It also curves in the air and will continue to curve after it bounces and skids when it lands. Unlike the fast cannonball serve, which can frequently be returned with a simple block, the slice serve requires a stroked return and, consequently, is more difficult for many players to handle than the flat serve.

1. John Alexander is in the ready position. Note that his front foot is angled toward the baseline to permit the ankle and the knee to accept the weight transfer onto the front leg. If the front foot is parallel to the baseline, the weight transfer is more difficult; thus good balance and body control are diminished. He has his front foot safely behind the baseline to be certain he will not footfault. His weight is on the front leg.

2. As he starts the service motion, he rocks his weight to the back leg. The tossing hand comes out to the right side of his body so that the ball can be tossed to the right. This is necessary for a good slice serve. The ball is in the fingertips and the palm of his hand is up, facing almost skyward.

3. The ball toss has been made to the right, and notice how his left arm has continued upward until fully extended. This helps him place the ball where he wants it. He has transferred the weight forward to the front leg and has brought the right leg forward slightly. I personally don't like bringing the back leg partially forward and "hitching," or hesitating with it before it continues forward. However, this didn't hinder a great server like Jack Kramer, and the pros will tell you it doesn't seem to hinder John's serve either. Note the position of his left foot, which is still the same as in the earlier pictures.

4. The left arm is starting down out of the way as the racquet starts to drop behind his back. He is watching the ball very closely. In this photo, as in the three previous ones, his knees are slightly bent. This enables John to have proper balance and good weight transfer from one leg to the other.

5. The left arm has dropped to permit a good shoulder rotation, and John has straightened his legs as he stretches up to hit the ball at his maximum reach. This will give him the best possible angle into the service court. The racquet head is "scratching his back," and the right elbow is high. He is still watching the ball very well. All his weight is on the ball of his left foot, enabling him to bring the right foot forward as he hits the serve.

6. The shoulders and hips have rotated as he reaches up to hit the ball. Thus he is able to have an unrestricted swing. He has gotten his body out of the way. He is leaning forward, fully extended, and has started to uncock his wrist at impact. His right leg is swinging forward, indicating he is getting his body weight into the serve, and he is still looking at the ball very carefully. The racquet face is approaching the ball at an angle indicating a slice serve. He is swinging across the back of the ball, and on contact the racquet face will then go around the side of the ball, creating the spin which is the slice serve.

7. After contact, the racquet continues to follow through, crossing the body from right to left. John has put all the weight onto the right leg, and his left foot has come off the ground from the force of his powerful swing and weight transfer. If John asked me to give him constructive criticism of this particular photo, I would point out three things: 1. The left arm is across the body, which makes the shoulder rotation more difficult. 2. If he didn't hitch the right foot (see photos 3, 4, 5), it would swing farther forward into the court. 3. In this way, his left foot would also not be so high off the ground or so far behind the baseline. Thus he could get a better start to the net.

8. John has completed the follow-through and is bringing the left leg down to make his next step toward the net. He is watching the ball go toward his opponent as he advances into the volleying position as quickly as he can. (Note: When I teach a beginner to serve, I try to teach him to keep the right leg back longer and then swing it forward as the weight transfers from the right leg to the left leg. This way the weight continues forward in one motion instead of stopping partway forward, as John's does. The right leg should come forward in much the same way it would if you threw a baseball.)

An Australian's View of the American Twist

by John Newcombe

The twist—or, as it's known, American twist—service is surely the most difficult serve to master, demanding more body and wrist action and a better sense of timing than either the slice or the flat serve. For that reason, I don't recommend that average players attempt to use it until they have the other two types of serves under control. But it is a weapon that all advanced players should make a part of their game.

To hit the twist, you bring the racquet sharply up and over the ball. This imparts a spin that causes the ball to loop over the net, then kick high to the opponent's left, pulling him out of position. One of the essential factors in creating this high-bouncing overspin is to finish the twist serve with the right arm on the right side of your body (the reverse for left-handers). This is a difficult maneuver and puts more strain on the back and arm than other serves, so it should be approached with caution. But if you will take the patience to learn this serve without putting undue stress on your body, it can be a valuable addition to your repertoire. For one thing, it is a better-percentage serve than the other two and so is more valuable on the second serve. Secondly, the bouncing action of the serve puts a lot of pressure on the receiver. The twist is especially useful in doubles because its looping action allows you more time to get to the net.

Most of the basics of good service form apply to the twist. I break these down into four parts:

1. The Ready Position

You should stand at the baseline with your feet placed properly—the front foot at a 45-degree angle to the net and the back foot just about parallel to the net (see frame 1 of the sequence on pages 86–87). They should be spaced comfortably apart. For the twist, you should use a Continental grip and, as you get ready, both hands should be out in front of you to permit you to balance and set yourself. It is important to set yourself slowly, and not to walk back to the baseline and toss up the ball straightaway. Every good player pauses before he begins to serve, and keeps his eye on the ball at all times.

2. The Backswing and Toss

The weight should be on your back foot as you begin your motion. Both arms begin their separate actions together. The racquet arm is moved back in a high arc (frames 2 to 5) with the wrist in a natural uncocked position until it is brought down behind the back.

The arm holding the ball, meanwhile, moves up in concert (frames 2 to 4). You should try to release the ball when the arm is at full stretch—although I must confess I seem to be doing it a bit prematurely in the accompanying sequence. One big difference between the twist and the other serves is that the ball should be tossed more to the left, almost behind your head (frame 5).

That, in turn, means you have to bend your body backward rather severely in order to hit the ball properly. This is necessary to give

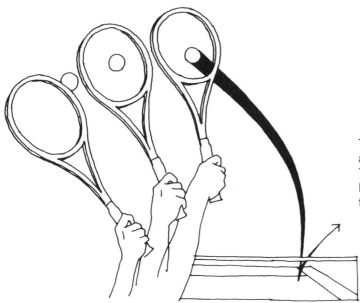

To hit a twist serve, the server snaps the racquet up and over the top of the ball with a very wristy action. This twisting action produces topspin and causes the ball to drop sharply as it crosses the net and kicks to your opponent's left side.

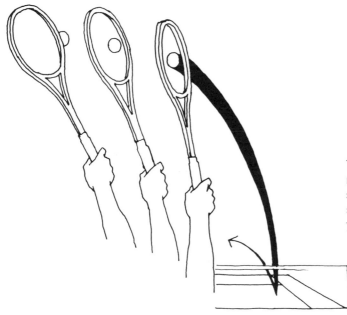

To hit the slice serve, contact is made slightly to the right of the center of the ball. The racquet head is snapped sharply forward and to the right so that a sidespin is imparted to make the ball curve off to your opponent's right side.

you the leverage for applying the twist you want to the ball.

3. Contact

From the "back-scratching" position in which your back is fully arched (frame 5), shift your weight to your front foot and bring your racquet straight up (frames 6 to 8). Its path is farther behind your head than it would be with the flat or the slice serve.

Your aim is to meet the ball (if you're right-handed) roughly at where 10 or 11 o'clock would be, assuming you were standing straight and the point directly above you represented 12 o'clock.

From here, your wrist does most of the work. As the racquet face strikes the ball (frame 8), you should snap your wrist and whip the racquet up and over the ball. Again, looking from behind you and putting a clock face on the ball, the racquet strings should make a line across the ball from approximately 7 to 1 o'clock. The racquet is swung entirely to the right, and forward almost not at all (frames 8 to 10). It is this whole action which puts the spin on the ball.

4. The Follow-through

To complete the sideways sweep of the racquet, pull it far to the right and then down to the right side of the body (frames 11 to 13). It doesn't cross over to the left side as it does in the other two serves. The shoulders, too, contradict the normal service action by still facing the right on the follow-through.

The object is to put the ball as deep into the other service court as you can. If it lands short, its high bounce makes it an easy target for a put-away shot by the receiver.

While the twist is a lethal serve, its singular motion does tip off the alert receiver that it's coming. When he sees the ball tossed almost directly behind the server's head, he can figure that the twist is on its way and prepare for a ball that will veer to the left.

The twist is not an easy serve to learn. The racquet must be brought across the ball at a very fine angle, with the edge of the racquet missing the ball by just a fraction. Not surprisingly, a player will commit a number of "wood shots" in the process of developing a twist serve. But it's a price that must be paid. Like any other shot, the twist serve takes practice, but it returns big dividends once it is perfected.

John Newcombe demonstrates the demanding twist serve. To get the twist action, Newcombe tosses the ball almost behind his head (frame 5) and snaps his racquet up and over the ball at contact (frames 8 to 10).

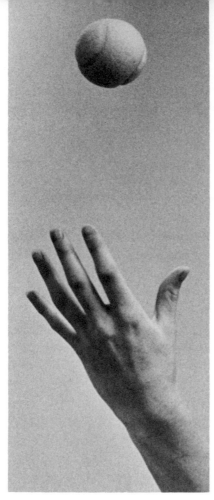

The Ball Toss
by Joe Brandi

The ball toss for a serve in tennis is one of those deceptively simple actions—like the free throw in basketball or the three-foot putt in golf. It looks easy and almost seems automatic—but how often we blow it!

If you want to develop an effective serve, though, the ball toss must become easy and almost automatic. How you toss the ball determines to a large degree how well you serve. If you can place the ball consistently at the right spot, you will be in a position to learn to serve with rhythm, power and accuracy. If you don't develop a good ball toss, on the other hand, you'll never develop a good serve. That's all there is to it.

The first rule of the ball toss is to keep things simple. Try to work on a clean, economical motion and not worry at the start about refinements. When you've mastered the basic toss, then you can begin to vary your motion for placement or special serves.

Let's start with how many balls you should hold in your hand. One or two? I know the conventional method is to hold two balls on the first serve. In fact, most of the top professionals do that.

But I don't recommend it. For one thing, the top professionals have bigger hands than average players—to say nothing of young novices, for whom holding two balls in one hand can be very difficult.

Secondly, think what happens when your first serve goes in if you start by holding two balls. Either you have to play the point while holding a ball in your nonracquet hand, a handicap at best, or you have to remember to throw it aside, a distraction you don't need.

And third, with the second ball right there in your hand you may tend to rush your second serve, instead of pausing to collect yourself as you should.

So when you begin to serve, keep that second ball in your pocket. And if you don't have a pocket in your tennis shorts or skirt, sew one on.

The one ball you take in your hand should be held lightly between the tips of the thumb and the index and middle fingers. Don't hold it in the palm of your hand, because that will

You should start your serve, as Brandi does here, with your racquet and ball in front of you about chest high (frame 1). Drop both your arms to thigh level (2), allowing your racquet arm to continue behind you in a sweeping arc. Your tossing arm will, simultaneously, come up in front of you with your arm outstretched (3). Release the ball gently as your arm passes a level just above the top of your head (4). The tossing arm will continue to follow through on the toss as the ball is placed in the air (5). The toss should reach its maximum height at about the highest point you can reach with your arm and racquet fully extended. That way you'll get maximum power as you hit the ball (6).

very probably cause you to kind of flick the ball aloft rather than place it up there gently.

Grip the ball lightly between the tips of the thumb and the two fingers. Don't squeeze the ball. Too tight a grip might put spin on the ball, which could result in a poor hit. Your grip should be gentle enough so that the ball will leave your hand with an imperceptible release of the fingers.

You should begin your serve with both the ball and the racquet held out in front of you about chest high. Start the tossing motion the instant you begin to swing your racquet arm down and back. Both arms should swing down together until your ball arm reaches your front thigh. At that point, your racquet should continue backward and upward in a large sweeping circle.

You should now, with a smooth motion, bring your ball arm upward almost in a straight line in front of you. Keep your arm outstretched as you bring it up.

The momentum of your rising arm should lift the ball from your fingertips just after your hand passes the level of the top of your head. Don't let go of the ball too soon, because then it will be harder to control; you'll tend to place it at a different point in the air each time you serve. The longer you can keep the ball in your hand, in fact, the better you'll be able to control the direction and height of the toss. It will also give you that split second longer to get your racquet around and up.

It's absolutely critical, of course, to place the ball at the right height and to be able to do it consistently. Too low and your serving motion will be cramped and awkward. Too high and the ball will be falling rapidly as you hit

it and your timing will suffer. Most advanced players toss the ball so that it stops at the exact height where the center of the racquet will be as they hit the ball.

But that's hard to do consistently. So I advise beginners and intermediate players to toss the ball about to the point where the top strings of the racquet will be when the serving arm and body are fully extended. That way you can be sure of always hitting your serve with your arm and body at full stretch even if the toss is a little lower than usual.

Determine how high the toss should be for you and practice tossing the ball to that exact height. If you have a garage or a room with a high ceiling, you can hang a small object at the height of your ideal toss and practice tossing the ball at that object until you can hit it softly at least nine times out of ten.

The ball should go slightly to your right (or left if you're a southpaw) and out in front of your body. Here's a handy way to check whether your direction is right. While you practice tossing the ball to the proper height, let it drop to the ground. It should land about a foot and a half in front of you and to the right (if you're right-handed) of your front foot.

I can't put too much emphasis on the value of practicing the ball toss. It's easy, I know, to shrug it off as too elementary to worry about and to work on something like ground strokes instead. But practice is the only way you'll ever learn to master the ball toss. Without a consistent ball toss, you'll never develop an effective serve. And without that, you'll never be as good at tennis as you can be.

Body Arc and Serving Power
by Bill Price

The serve is the most complex stroke in tennis and the stroke that allows for the greatest degree of personal idiosyncrasy. Ideally, each person should tailor his serving style to his individual build, strength and physical configuration.

If there is one characteristic that differentiates club players from professionals, it is the degree to which the knees and back flex during the serve. Most average players have a slight back arch when they serve, and this produces a generally adequate flat or slice serve. A powerful flat serve or stronger slice serve requires a high degree of flex—I call it the pro posture. And for the American twist service, an even more extreme flex is needed. Only then can you impart the necessary spin that gives the serve its characteristic high bounce.

The more you can comfortably increase your flex, the harder your serve will be. To appreciate the importance of back flex, con-

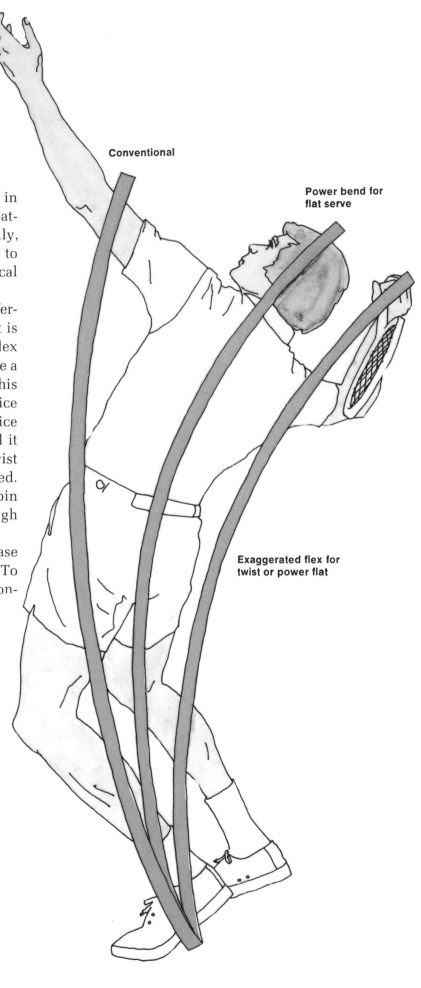

Conventional

Power bend for flat serve

Exaggerated flex for twist or power flat

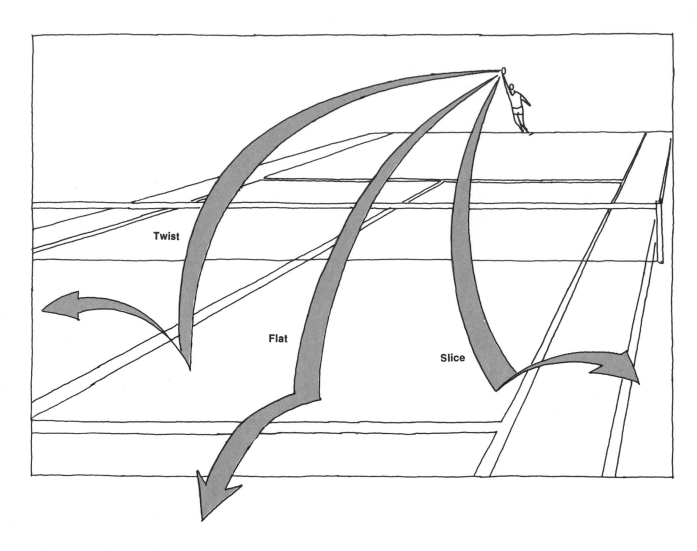

sider a pitcher and a catcher in baseball. The pitcher, with a big backward bend, can generate far more speed with his throw to the plate than the catcher can when he is standing erect and making a snap throw to second. So "bend" to the task a little more. Every player should strive to find his or her maximum comfortable bend.

How the Pros Serve
by John Alexander

The best servers on tour today, for my money, are John Newcombe, Arthur Ashe, Stan Smith, Nikki Pilic̆, Roger Taylor, Marty Riessen, Colin Dibley and Roscoe Tanner. Newcombe's is probably the best all-around serve, all things considered. He has a near-perfect, seldom-varying ball toss, from which he can hit a number of different serves—slice, flat or twist. His first ball is usually fast, flat and accurate, but he mixes it with an occasional twist to keep his opponents guessing. His second serve—the American twist—is consistent and deep. And, again, he mixes in an odd slice to keep his opponent from getting grooved. Smith's serve is very fast and he gets a lot of his first balls in, but I think it's overrated. Smith's serve is easier to handle, for instance, than Pilic̆'s, because Nikki's serve has more variety. On the other hand, Nikki's service form has its shortcomings too. The result is that he sometimes double-faults on crucial points. His ball toss, for one thing, is too low, and I don't think he watches the ball long enough before he makes contact.

When Ashe's flat serve is working well, it is one of the best in the game. Its speed comes from Arthur's long, fluid action and the snap he puts into his wrist, but it was faster before Arthur developed arm problems. Both Dibley and Tanner have remarkably fast flat serves, but Dibley hurts himself with double faults. Tanner's serve lacks variety and the toss lacks height, but when he's getting it in, it doesn't matter that much. Pancho Gonzalez, whose serve was once clocked at nearly 113 miles an hour, has said of Tanner's serve: "The form is almost perfect. He uncoils from the first movement. At impact he has his body fully extended, and he gets the full benefit from his swing. That, of course, contributes to the power he gets into the ball. So, too, does the speed of his swing. It is exceptionally fast. He gets his body out ahead of his racquet more than most top players, but manages to catch up by swinging the racquet faster than other players do."

Then there are Marty Riessen and Tom Gorman. Some people might be surprised that I mention them in the company of other big servers. But Marty's strength lies in the speed with which he hits his second serve, and Tom's in his excellent use of the twist.

As for the women, the most powerful server, I suppose, is the only player with a true flat first serve, and that's Virginia Wade, the English star. She has a very smooth action and leans into the serve to get as much body weight behind it as possible. True, she often misses on her first serve (as is the case with many flat servers), but she can back it up with an excellent American twist for her second serve. There is a lesson here: a player does not get to the top in the pro ranks with only one type of serve. The top players can produce all three of the principal variations—the flat, the slice and the twist—without becoming reliant on any one. Most pros use all types of serves and pull out the fast flat serve as an offensive weapon when the need arises for an ace or winner. Rosie Casals' service is a potent weapon too, especially when she employs her twist delivery.

The pro ranks are loaded with outstanding servers. Colin Dibley (far left) was clocked by *Tennis* magazine as having the fastest serve in tennis, but Roscoe Tanner (above left) isn't far behind. Tom Gorman's twist serve (below left) is a key ingredient in his success, and Marty Riessen's depth and control (below) give him one of the best second serves in tennis. Among the women pros, Virginia Wade (above) is generally conceded to have the strongest serve, but Rosie Casals' twist serve (right) is something special too.

Chapter 6 The Overhead

How to Hit the Overhead
by Fred Perry

If you have nightmares about your overhead smash and get butterflies in your stomach when you have to hit one, don't worry. Lots of players do—even some of the best. You're in good company.

You can usually tell how much the average player fears the overhead by the way he prepares for the shot. Most players look like old hens when the ball is way up in the air. Lots of fiddling and fussing. Feet all over the place. No balance. No idea what to do. Little wonder the percentage of misses and air balls is so high.

That it would pay the average player handsome dividends to take the time and trouble to develop an overhead is obvious. If you want to play the game seriously, or if you want to play the net at all, you must be able to hit the overhead consistently. If you don't, your opponent will lob you into submission. On the other hand, if you smash well, you will welcome those lobs eagerly. There is probably no greater satisfaction in tennis than taking a full-blooded crack at an overhead and putting it away for a resounding winner.

The "Jump Service"

For my money, the most effective way to hit the overhead is to hit it as if it were a "jump service." If you can get a mental picture of that, you're well on your way.

In preparing for a smash, early position is crucial. As soon as a lob is hit, you should be turning sideways to the net and skipping backward as speedily as possible with short overlapping steps. The weight should be on the balls of your feet as if, in fact, you were going to jump at any moment.

Getting the Arm Back

We have already established that the overhead motion resembles the serve. But there is one major difference. When you're getting set to hit an overhead, the backswing should be simpler and shorter than it is with the serve. Instead of winding up, you simply let the racquet head drop behind your shoulder in the so-called "back-scratching" position. The reason for this is that the lob is descending from a greater height than a service toss, and the shot requires much more precise timing.

It is important to stress that you should be in this position—sideways to the net, racquet back—even while you are positioning yourself to hit the ball. Ideally, you should hit the overhead from approximately the same position as you hit the service—above the right shoulder if you are right-handed, and slightly in front of you. Your opponent is not going to aim to put the ball there, so you have to get yourself into that position as quickly as possible. One way many pros line up the ball is to use their free hand to trace the flight of the ball.

The actual hitting of the overhead is nothing more, really, than a flat serve. Slicing the ball or trying to put spin on it in any way is unnecessary and risky. Make sure the racquet

Players with natural athletic ability and a flair for the dramatic—like Ilie Natase—generally excel on the overhead.

1. In this stop-action photo sequence, WCT professional and former Trinity University All-American Paul Gerken shows the proper form to be used in hitting an overhead. At the ready position, be prepared to receive a volley or to move back quickly for a lob. The racquet should be held up and forward.

2. As soon as your opponent sends up a lob, turn sideways and skip backward as rapidly as possible with short overlapping steps. It is vital to get the racquet back early while moving into position. Keep your eyes on the ball and be ready to make small adjustments in your position as the ball descends.

3. The overhead motion is very much like that of the serve but with a shorter backswing. Instead of using a large circular windup, let the racquet drop behind the shoulder in the "back-scratching" position. If you decide to jump for the smash, leave the ground off one foot and come down on the other.

4. Hit the overhead from approximately the same position as the serve—above the right shoulder and slightly in front (if you are right-handed). Be sure to make the racquet head move through the ball. If you don't hit through the ball, then you'll probably drag the ball down into the net.

5. The racquet has now come right through the ball. The correct action at this point should be exactly the motion you would use if you were trying to throw the racquet across the net. And keep your eyes on the ball all through the stroke, if possible. Resist the natural tendency to drop your head.

6. After an overhead, your follow-through should be as complete as if you had just served and you should be perfectly in balance, despite having jumped for the ball. It takes time to develop the timing and rhythm so necessary for the shot. But fluency should eventually come with practice.

head moves through the ball when you stroke it. A common mistake among the club players is to "drag" the ball into the net. If you can picture yourself throwing your racquet over the net, you can avoid this problem. It will also help to impress upon you the importance of follow-through.

On the Bounce

Some lobs are hit so high that it is usually more advisable to let them bounce, at least until you have gained so much confidence in your overhead that it doesn't matter to you.

Hitting such an overhead on a bounce can be tricky. Here again, positioning is the key. Most club players stand too far behind the point of the bounce. The right place to be is almost directly on the spot where you think the ball will land. Usually the trajectory of the ball after the bounce will carry it almost straight up. At this point you should jump to meet the ball with your racquet at the highest point that's comfortable for you, using the "jump service" technique I mentioned earlier. I can't overemphasize the importance of height. You should always get up as high as you can. And don't be afraid to hit the ball hard.

The Low Lob

Smashing the lower lob presents a different sort of problem. You can't afford to let it bounce, because it will scoot away from you on a hop. Instead, you have to move into a position under and behind and in the direct line of the flight. Here again, don't be timid. Get up there after it, swinging the racquet toward the ball with the same motion as in the normal overhead, so that you are well off the ground at the moment the racquet meets the ball. Hit through the ball, and make sure the follow-through is a long one.

The Case for Jumping

The reason I suggest that you learn to hit the "jumping" overhead should be obvious. Your ability to leap gives your opponent that much less passing room above you, and hitting the ball from height increases your power and hitting angle. It's not as hard a shot as it might seem. The key is to coordinate your movements. You don't jump and then swing the racquet. If you did, you'd probably break your neck. The jump and swing must be done simultaneously. The whole movement should be timed perfectly and executed with rhythm. Simply take your service stance. Then, as you start the racquet swinging, jump off the ground and complete the swing at the same time. Ideally, you should leave the ground off one foot and come down on the other.

The Backhand Smash

The backhand smash is far more difficult and much less decisive than the forehand smash. Given a choice, you should always hit the overhead from the forehand side, but if you are forced to make the difficult backhand smash, make sure that your right shoulder is turned well around behind the ball. This will give you the room you need to swing the racquet down and through the ball.

Since power is difficult to generate on a backhand smash, you should concentrate on accuracy. Rather than trying to put the ball away, try to put it in an awkward place so that you can put away the return. A last-minute turn of the wrist can produce some surprising angles. But be sure the wrist is firm at the moment of impact.

Be Decisive

The cardinal rule of the smash, especially the overhead, is to hit it decisively. Never be tentative. The smash was designed to be a winner. Your opponent should never get the feeling that you fear the shot. Establish your position early. Get up there after the ball and then give it a healthy crack. Balance and a good follow-through with the racquet head complete the picture—along with practice. Lots of practice. A good overhead has to be cultivated over a long period of time. Learning it requires long, often backbreaking work. You should always hit several during your warm-ups. If you are hesitant about it, it's unquestionably a matter of practice. Do it. Not to experience the thrill of pounding the daylights out of the ball is to miss one of the supreme delights of tennis.

Overheads the
Professional Way
by John Alexander

There isn't a professional on the circuit who does not have a reasonably strong overhead. Some are stronger than others, of course, but nobody can play tournament tennis unless he can combat the lob.

To hit the overhead well, you have to be fairly well coordinated and nimble on your feet. The shot demands sharp reflexes and top physical conditioning. Running quickly from net to baseline to position yourself for overheads several times in a match can tax your reserves.

Certainly one of the best overheads in tennis belongs to Stan Smith. Smith is a superbly conditioned athlete who, at 6′ 4″, can jump high enough to hit offensive smashes from just about anywhere on the court. With his long legs, he can run backward quite easily and is remarkably graceful as he leaps and twists to execute the smash.

You do not have to be as tall as Stan Smith to hit strong overheads. Tom Gorman is only about 5′ 10″ and has an excellent overhead. He has good athletic moves and he jumps well for his smashes. Chuck McKinley was only 5′ 8″ but, like Gorman, could jump well without losing balance or rhythm. McKinley added something extra by using plenty of wrist with the stroke. But I do not recommend that for the average player.

Even some pros have problems with the smash. Rod Laver, for instance, has a relatively weak smash—mainly because he has

back problems that make it difficult for him to stretch for the stroke. And Roscoe Tanner, who has one of the most powerful serves in the game, has a relatively poor smash. He doesn't seem to have any rhythm in the stroke.

Not long ago, Arthur Ashe had problems with his overhead. Arthur's solution was to go back to basics, and watching him illustrates well the fundamentals of the stroke—particularly the importance of getting the racquet back early. Arthur has an interesting habit of tracing the arc of the ball with his free hand. It obviously helps him to position himself better and is probably a good model for beginners to follow.

Apart from physical conditioning and the techniques outlined in the previous section, I can think of one more vital consideration for this stroke: keeping your eye on the ball. It may seem obvious, but many players—even pros—have trouble with the overhead because they fail to keep their eyes on the ball. You should not take your eyes off a lob for even a fraction of a second. Forget about your opponent's movements. Just concentrate on hitting the ball. Resist the tendency a lot of players have to duck your head and take your eyes off the ball just before the moment of impact. Stay with it all the way. The smash is a bold, aggressive stroke. Be bold with it in practice, and you will develop the confidence to use the smash in your matches.

Stan Smith's brilliant overhead (far left) is aided greatly by his height and superb athletic ability. It's not necessary to be tall, though, to smash well, as Tom Gorman (above, left) has demonstrated. Other leading players with exceptional overheads are Arthur Ashe (above) and Billie Jean King (below).

Chapter 7 The Lob

The How and Why of Lobbing
by Bob Harman

Many average players almost never lob. The shot is looked upon in some tennis circles as a "sissy stroke." But not in the pro ranks. The best of the big-time players lob very well. Just watch Ken Rosewall and Ilie Nastase, or younger players like Björn Borg, Jimmy Connors and Raul Ramírez. Virtually all of the true greats of tennis, from Bill Tilden and Suzanne Lenglen to Pancho Gonzalez and Maureen Connolly, would frequently pull out a lob at crucial points of important matches.

The lob is more than a defensive stroke to use only when you are in trouble. It can be a dangerous weapon, even against polished professionals. Against ordinary players, it can be positively decisive.

There are two types of lobs: defensive and offensive. The defensive lob is usually hit from behind the baseline or far out of the sidelines of the court. Its purpose is to rob your opponent of an easy kill at the net and to give you time to get back to position.

The offensive lob is generally hit from just inside the baseline. It is a good deal lower than the defensive lob (but high enough so that the opponent can't reach it) and can be particularly effective against a net rusher on return of service.

Interestingly enough, you use almost the same arm motion for both offensive and defensive lobs. The key difference is that you lift your racquet more gently—not more quickly—when hitting the offensive lob. Since you do not want the ball to go as high, you should not angle the racquet as sharply or stroke with quite the same degree of power as you would on a defensive lob. On the other hand, when you hit a high defensive lob you want to be sure to angle the ball upward and more steeply so that it lands in the court.

With both types of lobs, you stroke through the ball just as you do when hitting ground strokes. The difference, though, is that you lift as you stroke and follow through with a rising arm. The follow-through is extremely important. The biggest mistake average players make in lobbing is to hit the ball with a jerk, stopping the racquet too soon. The lob is best thought of as a smooth scoop shot.

Ron Holmberg, who was an excellent lobber when he was playing the circuit, recommends two stroking principles above all. "First of all," he says, "you must use a long, smooth stroke, trying to keep the ball on the racquet as long as possible, in order to get more control. Secondly, concentrate on getting the highest point of the lob directly above or slightly behind your opponent, depending on his position in the court."

The Anatomy of a Point-saving Lob
by Bill Price

In the stop-action sequence of photographs that follows, we see how Cliff Richey goes about extricating himself from trouble with a scrambling defensive lob—one of those impossible-looking shots that invariably bring oohs and aahs from the stands. Note that as desperate as the shot may be, Richey *strokes* it—he does not jab it, the way many club players do.

3. Racquet back.
After recovering his balance, Richey gets his racquet back with both hands, still looking as though he were about to make a normal ground stroke. For a good lob, you must use as much of your regular ground stroking as possible by assuming the proper position and lifting the ball high over the net.

1. Out of position.
Richey has just hit a passing shot that didn't pass and is now struggling to get back into a good defensive position. He appears to be off balance, but he knows that the bounce of the ball will give him enough time to prepare for a backhand defensive lob. This shot can also be used from the forehand, of course.

4. Hit it.
Both hands are still in contact with the racquet, which is well back, as it would be for a regular backhand with good power. This looks almost like the ground-stroke position except that the right leg is farther from the net than the left. It's necessary to take a full swing at the ball so that it will go high and yet travel almost the full length of the court.

2. Move to the ball. .
Now Richey has regained his balance nicely and is moving toward the ball. His left hand is still in contact with the racquet, just as it would be for a regular ground stroke, although by now he has decided that he is going to lob. If he hits the ball high and deep, his opponent will have to look at it for a long time, which might make it difficult to smash.

5. Aim for depth.
Despite his compromising position, Richey is getting about as much racquet on the ball as possible. This kind of full stroke will drive the ball perhaps 40 feet into the air. However, beware of the wind, particularly when the ball goes above fence level. The ball is not traveling as fast as in a normal ground stroke, which makes it more susceptible to wind.

6. Follow through.

Try for a complete follow-through when hitting the defensive lob. Here Richey has just hit the ball, but his follow-through is a little short because, despite the time gained by lobbing, he is still concerned about getting back into a good position for the next shot. When using the defensive lob you must make sure that the ball is on the upward part of its flight as it passes the net. The ball loses speed at the top of its flight and drops down more sharply than it goes up. If the ball is going up past the net, then it probably will fall close to your opponent's baseline.

7. Recovery.

The backhand defensive lob will most likely leave you in a poor position, facing away from the court. Richey is now beginning to spin around in order to get back into position. Be prepared for your opponent to return an overhead smash. Stay close to the baseline.

8. Ready for the return.

If your opponent smashes, the best position in which to receive the shot is probably about three feet behind the baseline, just as Richey is in this shot. His lob has given him time to get back onto equal terms with his opponent. As soon as he gets a short ball, he can move forward toward the net.

The Topspin Lob
by Rod Laver

I'm often asked the secret of competing against such powerful net players as John Newcombe and Stan Smith. One of the deadliest weapons against such over-powering net men is the heavily topspinning lob. This shot whips sharply over the head of the man at the net, drops rapidly in the back-court, bounces and snaps off toward the back fence like a startled jackrabbit. Your opponent is left scrambling down the court for an impossible get. The lob opens up the court, turning a defensive situation into an offensive position.

There is obvious satisfaction in hitting an effective topspin lob. It is a tough shot for your opponent to return, and it requires a high degree of stroking expertise, so that you'll feel pleased with your accomplishment. Unfortunately, the skill that's needed for an offensive topspin lob is difficult to obtain. I've been hitting it since I was 10 years old and I still muff the shot from time to time. It is fair to say that you should have a good topspin ground stroke before you attempt the lob. Unless you know that you can put plenty of spin on the ball, you will put up lobs that can easily be smashed back at you for outright winners. You'll want to avoid that mistake.

The topspin lob is easiest to stroke on slow surfaces, where the ball stands up relatively high so that the racquet can come under the flight of the ball, whip rapidly over it and then finish very high. You can use this stroke on fast-paced balls, but the average player will find medium- or slow-speed balls the easiest to handle. Unless your backhand is exceptionally strong, you should first try the topspin lob on your forehand.

The Essentials

As with any tennis stroke, you should begin with good footwork. You must quickly get side-on to the flight of the ball. Chances are that your opponent will be close to the net and you'll have to run for the ball. Even so, you should stop before you hit the ball. It is almost impossible to get the control needed for this stroke if you are running at the time you hit the ball.

As you begin to run for the ball, start your backswing at the same time. I recommend an almost straight backswing, with a looping forward swing that comes up underneath the flight of the ball. The general pattern of the swing is rather like an inverted half-moon, with the curve followed on the forward swing up to the point of contact with the ball. This swing closely resembles my conventional topspin forehand ground stroke, so that I can disguise the lob right up to the last second. That way, my opponent has less time to start his retreat from the net in order to prepare for a smash. Most top players can disguise both the type and the placement of their shots, but I don't think the average player should concern himself too much with that aspect of this shot. Just be sure you have a smoothly flowing looping action that comes up under the ball's path.

The forward swing for a topspin lob is one of the few situations in which it's permissible to drop your racquet head below the level of your hand, as I am doing in the high-speed photo sequence on pages 110 and 111. This occurs because I cock my wrist during the backswing and uncock the wrist at the point of impact so that the racquet head is moving very fast to put maximum topspin on the ball.

Hitting the Ball

You should contact the ball with the racquet face almost vertical and moving upward in a rapid flicking motion. However, it is not a brushing motion. You should hit *forward* and *through* the ball, but the racquet should momentarily grip the ball with an uncocking of your wrist and a turning of your forearm at the same time to create the topspin. You must have a firm grip to hit this shot. A slight mishit off center will cause the racquet to spin in your hand unless you grip the handle tightly. A badly mis-hit shot will cause you

to lose so much control that you'll probably slam the ball over the fence, just as I have done many times.

The critical points to remember about the impact are (1) you must uncock your wrist to speed the movement of the racquet head and (2) you must carry the ball on your racquet long enough to impart sufficient topspin. Carrying the ball like that requires that you have a good racquet feel. If not, you are going to need lots of practice with topspinning shots before you can develop the confidence you need for the lob.

I find it best to contact the ball just behind my front foot, about waist high. If you hit the ball too far in front of your body, you will be unable to get power into the shot, because you will be reaching for the ball and be unable to move the racquet head swiftly enough to get topspin. You will not need much weight transfer for this stroke. Most top pros do not put much weight into this shot, relying more on the topspin to carry the ball swiftly through the air. I generally hit this shot with my weight on my back foot, a practice that is often condemned by teaching pros. Nonetheless, hitting off my back foot helps me get the flicking action and assists me in continuing the follow-through upward before my arm comes across my body.

The follow-through should be as full as possible. After you hit the ball, your arm should come upward sharply and finish almost directly overhead, with your body open—that is, facing the net. I prefer to continue the follow-through across my body, although that is not as necessary for the topspin lob as it would be for a forehand ground stroke.

After completing the follow-through, you will usually have plenty of time to return to the center of the court in preparation for the next shot—assuming that your opponent has

In this high-speed photo sequence (above), I run into position and take my final steps just after the ball bounces (frames 2 and 3). My backswing has a slight loop to it and I cock my wrist as I complete the backswing (4). The racquet then comes forward in a low arc and begins to come up under the flight of the ball (5, 6, 7). At impact (8) my weight is on my back foot and the racquet is already moving swiftly upward. Keeping the racquet face open, I make contact with a rolling action of the wrist and forearm as the ball comes off the racquet (9, 10). The uncocking of my

wrist, which starts just before impact (see enlarged frame 8, opposite page), continues after impact, and my arm straightens out (enlarged frame 10, left) as I go into the follow-through (11, 12, 13). Note that my body has twisted around so that I am almost facing the net as I complete the stroke, although my feet are still in a closed stance. This twisting of the body helps me get the buggy-whip action that this stroke demands. The follow-through continues outward and upward (14) and finally finishes across my body (16). I follow through in the direction of the shot.

managed to return your lob. The topspin lob can be an outright winner, although I often use it to put my opponent off his net game and so secure an opening for a winning passing shot from his weak overhead return of my lob.

Where to Hit

When the opportunity arises, you should hit your lobs crosscourt, corner to corner. This will give you the maximum length and hence a little more margin for error. However, there's no reason why the topspin lob should not be hit down the line or down the middle of the court—especially in doubles, in which you should always aim your lobs over the head of the opposing net man. Direction is largely a question of timing the impact of the ball. Since I am left-handed, if I hit the ball a little in front of me, it will go to my right; if I hit the ball a little late, it will go to my left (for a right-hander, those directions will, of course, be reversed). No matter what direction you choose, you must still follow through completely in the direction of the line of flight that you intend. Initially you will find it easier to return the ball pretty much in the direction from which it came, but as you gain confidence, you will be able to place the shot as easily as a ground stroke.

Although the topspin lob is used sparingly in an actual match, it's a shot that needs plenty of practice. For practice you should have your partner hit medium-paced balls that bounce between the service line and the baseline. The balls should bounce at least waist high. I find that few average players can do this consistently, so I recommend that you use a ball machine if possible. You can adjust the machine to give the right speed and bounce every time so that you don't have to worry too much about running into position.

In practicing, make sure that you're side-on to the ball's flight, and remember to get your front foot out across your body before you hit. This allows you to uncoil your body as you make the stroke, helping you get the whippy action that the stroke demands. Cock your wrist during the backswing and uncock it with a rolling action as you impact the ball. After a few attempts you should start to put a little topspin on the ball and improve on that considerably as your confidence builds.

When you come to use the topspin lob in a match, there are three points that you should keep in mind:

1. Early preparation is essential for this shot. Get into position quickly and keep your eyes on the ball throughout the stroke.
2. Whip the racquet up and over the ball as quickly as possible, but keep the ball in the center of the racquet. If it rolls to the edge you'll have a double hit, most likely.
3. Don't abbreviate your follow-through. Follow the ball upward and forward in the desired direction of the shot.

Don't be discouraged if your first attempts to use this shot in match conditions lead to failure. You have to be well coordinated even to try the topspin lob. It is not a shot to try when your timing is slightly off or if you haven't practiced recently. Many of our students at Laver/Emerson Tennis Weeks ask to be taught this shot, but Roy Emerson and I advise its use only by players who already have an excellent ground-stroke repertoire.

Chapter 8 The Drop Shot

The Drop Shot
by Ron Holmberg

The drop shot is designed to land only a few feet or so beyond the net. The basic drop shot looks pretty much like a conventional forehand or backhand but is hit gently so that it lands just beyond the net. A good drop-shot artist can hit the ball from almost anywhere on the court and can sometimes put so much spin on the ball that it actually dies when it hits the ground, or even bounces back toward the net. Developing the "touch" that enables you to do this, though, takes years of practice. Average players would do well to concentrate mainly on getting the ball to land as close to the net as possible and not concern themselves too much with tricky spins.

Like the lob, the drop shot is generally hit for strategic reasons. One of its strategic purposes is to force a baseline player to come to the net. Another is to win the point when your opponent is standing deep and lacks either the time or the speed to reach the ball before it bounces a second time. Unfortunately, the shot is not too effective on hard-surface courts, where the bounce is generally high, but it's a good weapon to have on clay or grass.

The Mechanics

The best time to hit the drop shot is when your opponent is deep and hits a ball that is going to land inside your service line. This means that ordinarily, when you hit the shot, you'll be moving forward—which is to say, hitting an approach shot.

As with any approach shot, you should not run directly at the ball but should move in alongside it. You will have to slow up for the shot, which makes it rather like walking through the stroke. The important thing—and the thing that many players overlook—is that you should never hit a drop shot when you are standing still. If you run up, stop, make the shot and then try to continue, you will find it very hard to get moving again and almost certainly find yourself badly out of position should your opponent manage a successful return. Finally, as in all shots, your weight should always be moving into the ball.

Master of the drop shot, Ron Holmberg demonstrates here and on the following page the finesse of this difficult shot.

In execution of the shot, your preliminary motion is the same—backhand or forehand—as in any ground stroke. The racquet should be well back, its head above the level of where you intend to hit the ball. The racquet should then come down in an arc. Drop shots are most effective when hit on balls bouncing low in the service box. On high-bouncing balls, you have the choice of hitting either an approach shot deep or a drop shot. In neither case, though, should you telegraph the shot by reducing your backswing.

Now we come to the big difference between the drop shot and the normal stroke. It comes at the moment of impact. When hitting the drop shot, you have to tilt the racquet face back a bit and hit *under* the ball. You should also try to keep the ball on the racquet for as long as possible without actually carrying the ball. You hit it softly but with a firm grip, using a gentle pushing and lifting motion that hoists the ball into the air. Hit correctly, the drop shot will float through the air with enough velocity to clear the net but will land close enough to the net to give your opponent a good run for his money.

Backspin and Follow-through

Some top players use considerable underspin on drop shots. You generate more underspin by hitting *under* the ball. If you can do it and still get the ball over the net, fine. But it's not necessary. The important element of the stroke is the follow-through, which should follow the flight of the ball. I can't emphasize this point strongly enough. The follow-through of the drop-shot move should be in the direction of the spot where you want the ball to go. It should be as natural as possible, with a smooth and flowing motion to a finish

that's as natural as that of a normal ground stroke. By following through, you help ensure that the ball clears the net by at least a two- or three-foot margin. You should not try to skim the net by inches. Usually that kind of unnecessarily risky drop shot will simply end up in the net on your side of the court. Get a good trajectory on the ball, but hit it gently enough so that it lands in a shallow spot on your opponent's court.

Placing the Stroke

Most drop shots should be hit down the line. It is easier to hit a drop shot down the line than to hit it crosscourt, since the ball has less distance to travel for the down-the-line shot. The shorter the distance needed, the easier it is to judge the speed that has to be put into the stroke to get it to drop a few feet over the net. Accurate placement is largely a matter of turning your body sideways to the direction in which you want to hit and following through properly. Don't try to disguise the shot by turning your body in the opposite direction. This can lead to an error. The disguise inherent in the drop shot is its similarity to a ground stroke, not fake body position.

The fact that the drop shot can be disguised is, of course, a prime asset of this stroke, but you don't have to make a great effort to achieve the disguise. A good drop shot will look almost exactly like a ground stroke right up to the point of impact. Many beginning players tend to overplay the disguise. They try to fool their opponents by looking down the line on, say, a crosscourt shot. But this usually means taking one's eye off the ball, and nothing could be worse.

Also, don't attempt to make the drop shot

The mechanics of the drop shot are similar to those of any ground stroke except for the final moment (below left), when the racquet face is tilted back. Note the full follow-through.

The backhand drop shot is executed in the same way as the forehand. Contact should be made in front of the forward foot, and the racquet face should be slightly open as the ball is hit.

too good. Unless you try to hit the ball high enough to clear the net with a substantial margin of safety, you may try to cut it too fine, and hit it into the net. The drop shot is a percentage shot—that is to say, one that should always get over the net even if your execution is not perfect.

It takes experience and practice to develop the fine touch that enables you to get the ball just over the net consistently. You can't expect to hit effective drop shots as soon as you begin to learn this stroke. However, don't wait for the perfect situation every time. Try the shot and you'll develop the touch gradually. You may make mistakes in the early stages, but it is well worth spending the time to add this stroke to your repertoire.

How the Pros Exploit
the Drop Shot
by John Alexander

There is no doubt that the Europeans, because of their clay-court experience, are the true masters of the drop shot. Tom Okker, Nikki Pilič, Ilie Nastase and Manuel Orantes make best use of this shot. Pilič even has a tendency to overplay this stroke on the faster surfaces, with the result that he loses some points when he uses it. On clay, however, Pilič can be hard to beat with his skillful combination of ground strokes, drop shots and drop volleys.

Some of the younger players with solid baseline games, such as Jimmy Connors, also have good drop shots. Because of his two-handed backhand, Connors can disguise his strokes until the very last moment.

The slow clay courts of Europe have bred such masters of the drop shot as Ilie Nastase (left) of Rumania, Nikki Pilič (above) of Yugoslavia and Tom Okker (below) of the Netherlands.

For an effective drop shot, you need lots of control. That's where the spin artists come into their own. Manuel Santana has a terrific backspin drop shot which curls over the net and then bounces straight back into the net or even back over the net again. You can imagine how tough it is to return that kind of devastating shot.

The drop shot can be used to good effect to tire your opponent by making him run up to the net frequently. I remember a match in the Italian Championships some years ago in which a consummate drop-shot artist, Beppe Merlo, was himself drop-shotted out of the match by another master of the stroke, Sergio Tacchini.

Late in the match, Merlo began to suffer from leg cramps, but he refused to give up the match. As play continued, Tacchini lobbed deep, forcing Merlo back to the baseline. Although Merlo managed a passably good return, Tacchini dealt him an angled drop shot that barely plopped over the net. In obvious agony, Merlo attempted to run for the net but collapsed before reaching the ball.

Tacchini, exasperated by the various delays caused by Merlo's cramps, rushed over to the net, wound it down and marched off the court with it under his arm. The Italian crowd was outraged, but Tacchini managed to escape with both the net and the match—and his skin!

Many players feel that the best counter to the drop shot is to drop-shot right back. I don't. I like to return a drop shot down the line as deep and low as possible. By playing down the line, I reduce the amount of empty court that will be open for a passing shot from my opponent. If I were to return the drop shot crosscourt, my opponent would have a wider angle available to him for his return. Only on rare occasions can a drop shot be returned crosscourt for an absolute winner. To my way of thinking, the drop shot can be used most effectively in mixed doubles to draw the opposing woman close to the net, where she can be smashed rather devastatingly. I must admit that this tactic sounds rather ungallant, and it does not, to be sure, find much favor among the mixed-doubles teams I have encountered. It does, however, demonstrate the basic usefulness of the drop shot.

There are relatively few occasions in which the drop shot can be used for an outright winner. On the appropriate surface, however, the shot can be used to set up a situation in which the next stroke will be a winner.

Chapter 9 The Return of Service

What You Need to Know About Returning Service
by Jan Kodeš

The return of service is probably the most underrated stroke in tennis. I can't think of any stroke that is practiced less. Yet when you consider that you must make this shot on approximately half the points you play, you can understand why I consider it, next to the serve, the second most important shot in the game.

To be sure, the return of service is not a specific stroke but rather a shot in which any number of strokes—backhand, forehand, lob, drop shot, etc.—may be called upon to do the job. In this regard, it is very much a strategic shot, a matter of planning ahead and choosing. I like to think of returning serve as rather like chess. Both you and the server have time to get set, to anticipate the next move and to plan a few moves ahead. Like a chess player, you know—or quickly get to know—your opponent's tactics in serving and his actions immediately afterward. Hence you need a plan for the return which you can carry out no matter what type of ball you are receiving.

When I face a top player like Stan Smith, I plan each return of serve differently. This keeps the pressure on and, hopefully, forces a break of serve. You can do the same in your weekend matches.

The Waiting Position

To return service effectively, you have to be standing in the right position. But there is no one "right" position. Rather, your position de-

pends on what your strongest stroke for a return is and the kind of serves you expect from your opponent. Since I normally favor my backhand, I cover my forehand more; that is, I move closer to the singles sideline when receiving in the deuce court. Generally, in singles, I recommend standing on the baseline (or a few feet behind the baseline against a strong server). Stand a couple of feet from the singles sideline if the server is a right-hander. For a left-handed server, move a little farther to the left—especially when you are

Jan Kodeš demonstrates tennis' second most important shot.

In singles, the receiver should be standing close to the baseline while awaiting serve and should have a plan of action in mind.

Try to meet the ball, if possible, waist high and out in front of the body to get the proper control and power on the shot.

Watch the ball from the moment the server begins his toss, and be prepared to move after his delivery with rapid strides.

An open stroking stance is sometimes necessary, though never desirable, in order to retrieve a really fast serve.

receiving in the ad court, where a lefty can serve wide.

Having taken the proper position, you can now plan your next move. Although I often go for a winner on return of serve, especially when I am opposing a player whose game I know well, I don't recommend this for average players. Your chief objective should be to keep the ball in play. You should plan a conservative return. Then you can decide on the basis of what your opponent does with your return whether or not to go on the attack.

The Surface Factor

Much of what you plan to do with your return of serve will depend on the surface you are playing on. If you are playing on a slow surface, like clay, the chances are your opponent is not going to come into the net behind his serve. In this situation, I recommend as deep a return as possible, either crosscourt or down the line. On faster surfaces, where the opponent is charging, you are better off trying for a relatively low and angled shot—one that cannot be volleyed easily. This is what I mean by planning ahead. Even before the ball is served, you should have an idea in your mind of what you're going to do with the ball.

Anticipating the Serve

Once you have a plan of action firmly fixed in your mind, you can turn your attention to the server. Assuming you know his tactics well, you will probably be able to guess whether the serve will be to your forehand or your backhand and be able to start your backswing that fraction of a second earlier. If you are facing a new opponent, observe him carefully for the first few games and play it conservatively until you have a good fix on his serving tactics.

Watch especially where he throws the ball. By noting whether the ball goes to the right or the left, you often can tell whether a serve will be coming down the center or wide across the court. Watching the server and not the ball is a common mistake of inexperienced players. Once you see the server's ball arm go up, fix your eyes on the ball and keep your eyes on it until the point is finished.

The Correct Grip

Everybody seems to have a different theory as to which grip you should use when awaiting serve. I use the Continental grip for all my shots, forehand or backhand, so obviously I favor it for returning service too. If you use different grips for backhand and forehand, I think you should assume the grip for whichever of the two strokes—backhand or forehand—is your stronger. Be prepared, though, to switch grips once you see the ball coming to the other side.

You should make that decision about switching as soon as you can after the ball leaves the opponent's racquet. You are shifting grips as your racquet moves back. Make sure you get the racquet back early. Every fraction of a second you gain in getting the racquet back will help you execute this stroke better, particularly on fast surfaces like grass and concrete.

Hitting in Front

A key to hitting return of service well is to make contact with the ball well in front of your body. Against a fast server, this requires very quick reactions. Quick reactions, in turn, depend on proper body balance so that you can move easily in the same direction as the ball. Don't make the mistake of many players who stand with their weight back. Instead, be waiting in a slightly crouched position, with your weight forward and on your toes. I crouch more than most players on return of serve, but then I bounce in the air as the ball is served, so that I'm really on my toes to move to the ball.

If you want to hit the ball in front, you may have to cut down somewhat on your backswing. Don't worry about it. Take only as much of a backswing as you can without rushing the shot. Even if you have to abbreviate your backswing, don't stint on the follow-through. Try to carry the ball on your racquet as long as possible and then follow through out and forward, keeping your eye on the ball. As long as your weight is moving forward when you connect, the abbreviated backswing won't matter too much.

Not all serves can be returned the same way. On fast surfaces, where the bounce is low, you don't have time for much of a backswing at all. On clay, though, where the bounce is higher, you should have more time for a longer backswing and be able to hit a more conventional and powerful ground stroke. Yet even high-bouncing balls can be a big problem. Tom Gorman, for instance, has a high-bouncing second serve that is very difficult to attack. You don't have much choice on that sort of serve. You simply have to stay back and make sure you don't give him a return that's easy to volley back for a winner.

Varying the Return

Unless you are a skilled player, I suggest that you stick to the usual forehand and backhand ground strokes, modified as I have described, for the return of serve. The more advanced player, however, can often put the drop shot to good use for service returns. I favor using the drop shot as a surprise weapon on relatively slow courts, particularly if my opponent is staying back after his serve.

Sometimes the drop shot can be an outright winner. Often you can use it to set up a situation in which your next move will be a winning passing shot. It is part of the planning of the return of serve—the chess game I mentioned earlier.

Similarly, I feel that only a good player should run around a serve so that he can hit his strongest shot. It can be effective as a surprise when the server is expecting, say, a forehand return and he gets a backhand. But to run around either your forehand or your backhand calls for great agility and confidence in your timing and reflexes. Even the top pros only do it occasionally during a match. John Newcombe, for example, generally runs around the serve to capitalize on his lethal forehand, but only when the serve is aimed pretty directly at him, and not really well onto his backhand side.

Developing an effective return of serve is a matter of experience and intelligence. While you are getting the experience, there are three things I suggest you keep uppermost in your mind:

First, watch the ball from the moment it leaves the server's hand.

Second, lean into the stroke and hit the ball out in front of you for both control and power.

And finally, remember that the idea behind returning serve is to keep the ball in play. Stick with the high-percentage shots you know you can make well; resist the temptation to try for impossible winners.

How the Pros Return Service
by John Alexander

In discussing service returns, the moral I might draw from the pro players' realm is: Make the most of what you've got. Let me explain.

Some professional players have games built around the service return—notably Ken Rosewall, Rod Laver, Jimmy Connors and Jan Kodes. These four vary a great deal in approach. Rosewall's attitude might be considered defensive, for it appears that he rarely attempts a winning service return. However, he applies great pressure by returning a very high percentage of serves; his returns are rarely hit with great pace, but all are hit with purpose. Seldom does a Rosewall return go down the center of the court; it is usually aimed at a sideline. Therefore, although Ken's return is generally considered the best in the game, its real strength is not that it is an outright winner but that he is consistently faced with an easier second shot, his opponent already being drawn to one side of the court.

Laver's return is a very different matter. He has an infinite variety of returns, and when they are all working, his opponents find it impossible to settle down. Serve wide to Laver's backhand in the deuce court (which is not the best place to serve to Laver) and he has a perfect return—in six varieties. His three most noted are his full-swing topspin backhand—down the line and crosscourt—and a very sharply angled crosscourt chip. He also has a moderately angled crosscourt chip which usually lands very close to the sideline a little deeper than the service line. He has a full-

blooded backhand that can really give you shock. And, there is his punishing slice return down the line, a softer version of which will draw you a little too close to the net for comfort.

Kodeš's returns, although very good, do not have the variety of Laver's or the accuracy of Rosewall's. However, he consistently hits the ball back very hard, which is disheartening when you have thrown all you have at him.

Then there is Jimmy Connors. Connors has what many players consider *the* number one return of service in tennis. Unfortunately for the average player, Connors doesn't do anything special with the return that could serve as a model. He simply has fantastic powers of concentration, *sees* the ball remarkably well and has such a fine sense of timing that he can often return the most sharply hit serves back for clean winners.

Among the many excellent serve-volley exponents around the world, it's important to realize that Arthur Ashe, John Newcombe and Pancho Gonzalez, to name three, would be far lesser players were it not for their individualistic and very effective service returns.

Ashe returns similarly to Kodeš, possibly more brilliantly but not as consistently. The lack of consistency of Arthur's returns is not a weakness, however. People watching Arthur often say critically, "He's playing terribly. Why, he didn't even return one ball last game!" However, to his opponent Arthur's inconsistency can be very off-putting, especially when the next time he's receiving, he drills four serves back for the break. What he has actually done is break your serve-volley rhythm. When you're confronted with a regular flow of good returns, it almost feels unnatural to do anything but serve.

Newcombe as a young player was (and is now) a very strong serve-volley player, but he was not successful until he developed a receiving game. He did this by making the most of what he had. As his backhand is his weaker side, he does not try for more than he is capable of. Like Rosewall, he is not devastating, but consistent. Newcombe's most effective play to break serve is to move around weaker services and punish them with his superior forehand. This gives him a greater opportunity to knock off the next shot—if there is one.

Pancho's returns now are very similar to Rosewall's but even more defensive. He tries to play all his returns soft and low, the idea

being to limit the power of his opponent's volley. This gives Pancho a better chance to cover the next shot. This is sound thinking for someone whom we expect to slow up any century now.

Players with natural agility and well-developed ground strokes—like Ilie Nastase (left), Jimmy Connors (below) and Ken Rosewall (right)—have the best service returns for countering today's hard servers. Although serves are slower in the women's game, players such as Nancy Gunter (far right, above) and Chris Evert (far right, below) also owe their effective service returns to well-polished ground strokes.

PART II
Strategies

Chapter 10 Ground-stroke Strategy

Putting the Power
Forehand to Work
by Jack Kramer and
John Alexander

Back in the days when Bill Tilden and Ellsworth Vines were the kings of the game, the strategy for most big hitters was a kind of 1-2-3 tennis. Vines explained it this way: He would hit a hard forehand shot crosscourt. If it came back, he would then hit it hard down the line. If it came back again, he would hit it crosscourt. If it came back still another time, as he put it, "Then I knew I was playing one heck of a player." In other words, in those days you had to hit three good shots to win a point.

Today's players have a different style. Most of the strong hitters shoot for one big forehand down the line and go to the net immediately. This approach to tennis is frequently referred to as the "power game."

But simply being able to pound deep, strong forehands over the net is not enough. Just as important as power is the ability to place the ball where you want it: to hit it crosscourt or down the line; to hit it deep or angled. Above all, there is consistency. The forehand should be an attacking stroke, but nothing is more dispiriting to a player than to lose points when he is trying to take the offensive.

Specific Strategies

Assuming you have good control of your forehand, you should be able to use the stroke to control the ebb and flow of your rallies. It is possible, indeed probable, that your opponent will concentrate on your backhand (assuming that your backhand is weaker than your forehand), but there are limits to this strategy. For instance, on balls that are hit slowly and land short, you can generally pick the side, forehand or backhand, from which you want to hit. This is particularly true on the serve. Some professionals will tell you that it is bad practice to run around your backhand, but many of the best players do it, including John Newcombe and Charlie Pasarell. It isn't that these players have weak backhands. Rather, they have such confidence in their forehands that they try to attack with them at every opportunity.

Another problem for players with a strong forehand is what to do with the short ball hit to the forehand side. You'd be surprised at the number of professionals who have trouble with this shot. Jimmy Connors, for one, had a tendency early in his career to rush this shot, and his errors on the short forehand were the prime cause of his defeat by Alex Metreveli in the 1973 Wimbledon quarterfinals. "There's always the temptation to do too much with the shot," Connors says. "Now instead of trying to kill the ball every time, I find I can be just as successful with it if I angle or hit a little drop-shot return."

One strategy that helps enormously on short balls hit to the forehand is to have an idea ahead of time where you want to place the ball. Most of the top players on the circuit place short forehands down the line unless the other side of the court is wide open. There are good reasons behind this strategy. For one thing, knowing in advance where you will hit the ball reduces the chance of error that results from either indecision or too much thinking. Secondly, the fact that you can hit down the line a fraction later than you can hit crosscourt gives you more time to prepare—a key consideration on balls that require running on your part. Also, hitting crosscourt frequently means hitting on the run; the down-the-line shot often gives you the chance to plant your feet firmly and hit a full stroke.

Whatever strategy you use, never lose sight of the paramount principle in tennis: consistency. All the beautiful forehand winners you may hit during a match will amount, in the end, to zero if you make an equal number of errors.

Ground-stroke Development

Consistency is a matter of practice—the right kind of practice. When you're warming up your forehand, don't just hit the ball back to the middle of the court; place your shots all over the court. Hit some crosscourt, down the line, short and long. Try, if you can, to hit them all with the same general motion. That is what made Segura so tough. You never knew until the last second where he was going to hit the ball.

If you can develop an *aggressive* forehand at the same time you develop a *consistent* forehand, you will be a tough player to beat in any league.

The Thinking Man's Backhand
by Vic Seixas

Some players are lucky enough to have backhands so powerful they don't have to worry much about the subtleties of the stroke. Don Budge was such a player, and Tony Trabert was another. Although both of these players were astute students of tennis, neither had to rely much on cunning. They could practically blow opponents off the court with their lethal, flowing backhands.

Most players are not blessed with this blend of skill and power and need something else. In many cases, that something can be strategy. You should, of course, practice and develop your stroke as best you can. At the same time, don't ignore the mental aspects of the stroke, because those can help you develop an all-court game that opponents will respect.

The Power of Offensive Thinking

Whether or not you use topspin or underspin, or both, one key to an effective backhand is to think offensively as much as you can. If you have a choice, don't try to simply keep the ball in play in hopes that you will be able to maneuver it to your forehand sooner or later. The odds are that your opponent will wise up to this ploy and keep firing at your backhand.

Assuming that you have a respectable if not overpowering backhand, the next thing to keep in mind is to vary your shots as much as possible. Don't let your backhand become predictable. I've always tried to keep my opponent off balance with a chip shot here, a lob there and an angle shot another time. It prevents him from getting grooved and from camping in one spot waiting to pounce on a return.

The Backhand Return of Serve

Now for specific situations. Let's first examine the return of serve. In most better club competition, well over half of the serves in the deuce court come to the backhand side for right-handers—mainly because that reduces the available angles on a return. In the ad court, the right-hand backhand also gets a greater play, probably because most servers figure, correctly, that it is the weaker side.

Sometimes the receiver can try for an outright winner on a backhand return. But ordinarily, the percentages are against him. If the server is charging the net, the best strategy is to play for the next shot by attempting a low return that will land at his feet. That forces the opponent to hit up on your return and may set up an easy winner.

If, on the other hand, your opponent does not follow his serve to the net, hit your backhand as deep into his court as you can to keep him back and to nullify his advantage as a server. If possible, direct your return to his weaker side.

A further countermeasure is the element of surprise. Instead of playing safe, lash out with an attempted winner every once in a while. It may not succeed, but it will certainly give your opponent something to think about and may upset his rhythm.

Whether serving or receiving, when you approach the net and find yourself in a position for a backhand volley, be aggressive about it. Go for the winner. It may not always work out for you, but you should at least approach your shots that way.

The Backhand in Doubles

In doubles play, one strategy question is where the player with the stronger backhand should play when both partners are right-handers. Some say the stronger player should play on the right, so that he'll be in position to cover the middle of the court, where most shots are played. I disagree. As I see it, the partner with the stronger backhand should be on the left side, so that his backhand can handle the difficult sideline shots and, most particularly, the service returns in that court. He still has his forehand to cover the middle of the court.

Above all, don't be afraid of the backhand. If you work on your stroking and try to think offensively on court, the backhand can become an effective tool for you.

How to Win with a Zone Offense

by Charles Lundgren

Theoretically, every shot you hit in a tennis match should have a purpose. But that purpose is not always to win the point on that shot. On the contrary, most of the shots—especially ground strokes—you hit in a tennis match are designed not to win the point but mainly to increase the likelihood of your winning the point at a later time during the exchange. And a major factor in this strategy is where you happen to be on the court when you hit the stroke.

To illustrate what I mean, it might help for you to think of a tennis court as divided into three distinct areas: the backcourt, midcourt and forecourt (see illustration). Each of these areas has distinct strategic significance. The backcourt may be thought of as the unbalancing zone, the midcourt as the attack zone and the forecourt as the knockout zone.

Let's start with the backcourt, or unbalancing zone. Ideally, all your shots hit from here should be aimed at unbalancing your opponent. They should force him to fall backward, lunge to the side or get his feet into the wrong position, all with the idea of forcing a weak return or no return at all. If the latter results, the point is won. If he returns weakly, you are then in a position to adopt attacking strategy.

At midcourt, the attack zone, the knowledgeable player doesn't necessarily try to end the point right there. Instead, he tries to hit a deep, forceful but careful shot that *may* win the point but, more likely, will force the opponent into an anemic return that can be handled with ease at the net. Hitting the ball hard is not the only way you can accomplish this. Sometimes a high looping shot that lands

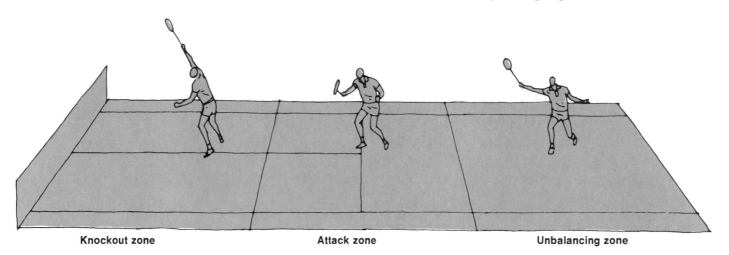

Knockout zone　　　　**Attack zone**　　　　**Unbalancing zone**

The court area from which you hit should determine your strategy. The back section should be thought of as the unbalancing zone, the middle section the attack zone and the net section the knockout zone.

deep in a corner is more effective than a bullet.

This brings us to forecourt shots—those at the net. The forecourt is the knockout zone. Overheads or volleys hit within this area should be hit with one purpose: to win the point. This can be accomplished in one of two ways: by hitting deep and fast to the corner, or by hitting short, angled shots away from your opponent. Your ability to do this, in many cases, will be determined by how strategically you have played shots hit in the unbalancing and attacking zones. Think about this "zone" approach to tennis strategy the next time you play. Let the zone dictate whether you try simply to unbalance your opponent or try for the knockout.

Chapter 11 Volley Strategy

Winning Tactics with the Volley
by Bob Harman

The strategic value of volleying should be obvious—not only in doubles, in which at least half your shots will be volleys, but in singles too. For if you never take the net in singles, you're handicapping yourself needlessly. For one thing, you put yourself at a disadvantage on short shots. To hit a short ball and then turn tail and scurry back toward the baseline is hard on the legs, and not very good strategy, either. Secondly, if you never take the net behind your serve, you allow your opponent to hit unpressured returns. You do not have to be a fierce slugger to volley effectively. Mainly it's a question of knowing how to seize the net comfortably, without sprinting, and where to place your volleys when you come to the net.

Getting to the Net

One of the best opportunities for seizing the net comes during your serve. A deep serve, hit into the corner, should give you time enough to get to the service line before the ball comes back at you. You don't have to sprint. Just glide. Take long strides with your feet close to the ground. Low steps save energy and get you there sooner.

The way to advance to the net is at a diagonal, following the direction of your serve. The center of the net is *not* your objective. Obviously you can't cover the entire court, but neither can your opponent pass you anywhere he chooses and still keep the ball in the court. A lot depends on where your opponent is standing. If he's standing, for example, in the corner of the ad court, he will have trouble keeping any sharply angled crosscourt shot inside the court. So even if you move to the middle of the ad side of the court, you're not really leaving the entire other side of the net unguarded.

As you glide toward the net to make the first volley, keep clearly in mind what you plan to do. Ideally, you want to volley deep to the corner as low as you can. Either corner will do. Usually it is best to volley to the opposite corner from the one you served into, since this will make your opponent run farther. But play it safe. There is no need to hit with spectacular speed and accuracy. Your first volley hit from barely halfway between baseline and net won't beat an average opponent even if you place it perfectly; he will have time to get to it. So why increase your margin of error by attempting a flashy shot? Just concentrate on a safe, deliberate volley, aimed well inside the corner. Keep it low, because if the ball bounces waist high your opponent has a good chance to wallop it back past you. You want to make him hit the ball up to you. Be ready once you have hit the first volley; don't wait to see where it's going. This is one of the commonest faults in weekend tennis. Get your racquet up to the ready position and glide in closer to the net. Your plan for the second volley should be simply to block it off, shallow and sharply angled, into the other service court—i.e., the opposite service court from where your opponent returned your first volley.

This sequence of two volleys, if executed well, will almost always win the point for you. First deep and low to one corner; then shallow to the other side, pulling your opponent far out of court. If you're up against a scrambler who manages to get the ball back, you can easily tap it away to the other side. Sometimes you can vary the sequence by crossing up such a scrambler and placing your next volley right back to the same corner, behind him as he is instinctively trying to scramble back to the other corner. But in any and all cases, do not become overeager and swat at the ball. If you do, you will probably flub your volley.

Volleying in Doubles

In doubles, the strategy of the volley is even simpler. Your first volley should always be hit crosscourt as deep as possible—unless your opponent has raced into position to volley. Make your shot as low as possible, so that he will have to scoop the ball up instead of lining it back for a passing shot.

If you have hit the first volley as you planned, you should move in a couple of feet closer to the net, ready for yet another crosscourt shot. You are forcing your opponents backward into a predicament in which they will have to hit the ball up. When that happens, and you get your chance to volley a rising ball, you can easily aim it wherever the opposition isn't.

If your opponents are adversaries worthy of their mettle, they will keep sending you low balls when you are in the forecourt. Just keep volleying low and crosscourt in return, until you get a chance to hit one downward. Stay far enough from the net so that you can get back to cover a lob in your half of the court.

Singles or doubles, always remember that the common blunder and cardinal sin of the volleyer is trying too hard to put the ball away. Most players make errors at the net by trying to force a kill when they are not really in position to make one. And they tire themselves out by hitting harder than they need to do.

The only time to hit hard at the net is when you are shooting for a small opening. When you can hit down at the ball from a spot near the net, you can simply block if off to one sideline or the other, irking your antagonists because of the ease with which you maneuver them around.

A good volley starts the instant after you hit the previous shot. Without waiting to see what happens to it, you must quickly get your body balanced and racquet in front of you again, ready for either a backhand or a forehand volley. Then you'll have that extra split second to lean forward and make your volley a stabbing thrust, with a firm wrist, as if you were spearing the ball. You can easily aim your shot by tilting your racquet.

The Surprise Volley

Many players overlook the chance to hit a surprise volley. The opportunity comes fairly often in singles, occasionally in doubles. It is useful for those who prefer to stay in the backcourt most of the time, although a tigerish player can use it just as readily.

The chance can arise during a long baseline rally. If your opponent has found a comfortable rhythm and is driving deep to you

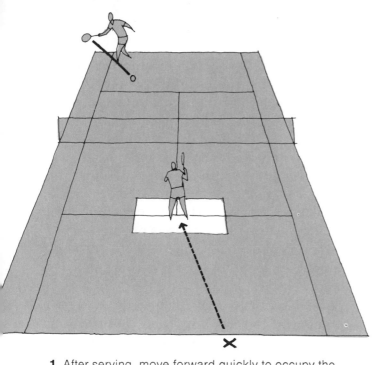

1. After serving, move forward quickly to occupy the center of a small area within which you can safely receive the opponent's return.

2. Hit the first volley deliberately, aiming it deep into the corner of the other side of the court. Keep it as low as possible.

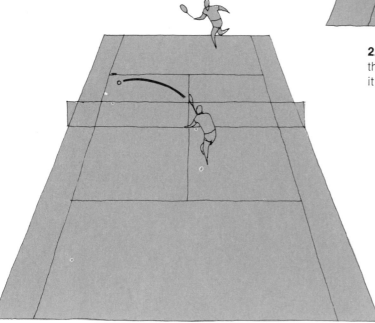

3. If the opponent returns the first volley, polish off the point with a sharply angled second volley back into the original service court.

Volley Strategy **137**

with maddening monotony, you can startle him out of his shoes by hitting the ball on the fly instead of waiting for it to bounce near the baseline.

I don't mean you should rush the net. After a deep drive of your own, just take a few stealthy steps over the baseline, into what is so often called no-man's-land—although you can own it if you know when to take possession. It is as easy to volley from here as it is from the forecourt. Your shot will get to your opponent much sooner than he expects, and his return will be shallower than usual. This allows you to creep in closer and volley again, usually for a winner.

The volley is an aggressive, offensive shot—especially in singles. But even if you play a prudent backcourt game in singles because you prefer not to run yourself into a frazzle, you can still sneak languidly up to the net with malice aforethought. Here's how.

A lob or a slow, high-arching drive that takes longer than usual to reach your opponent will give you plenty of time to amble up at least as far as the service line, and maybe farther. If you have stroked the ball to your opponent's forehand corner and he returns it down the line, you should plan on making your next shot a backhand volley, deep and low to the other corner. Conversely, if your lob or drive goes to his backhand, your volley should go to his forehand corner. In other words, your strategy is to volley toward whichever corner is farther from him.

Don't try to win the point with this first volley. A smart player scores many more points by outmaneuvering his opponent than by overpowering him. Here is one of the situations in which you can deliberately work him out of position by a planned sequence of shots.

After your first volley (deep and low, near a corner) you can move in a few feet closer to the net. The ball will probably come back to you on the rise.

Don't try to murder it. Just stick your racquet up, angled toward the side, so that the ball drops in very shallow territory and bounces wide out of court. This one-two sequence of a deep volley to one corner and a shallow volley to the other side will run the legs off your opponent, while you stand and gloat as you wait to put away another weak return. Whether it takes two or three shots as you approach the net, you won't even be breathing hard. What could be sweeter?

How to Cure Your Fear of the Net

by Charles Lundgren

All too many club players shun the volley for one very simple reason: fear. They are reluctant to come to the net because they are afraid they might be hit by the ball.

Fear of the ball at net is understandable. Self-preservation is a primary instinct in all of us. But this fear can be overcome if the player understands some basic facts.

First, assuming you had a baseball glove, you could probably catch most shots hit to you at the net. If you can catch the ball, the odds are that you can hit it. In fact, one way to conquer fear of the net is to stand up there holding the racquet straight up and down and letting the approaching ball simply bounce off the racquet head. Then, as confidence increases, a short forward punch can be used, and later, a slight backswing can be added.

Secondly, while there is less time to react to the ball when you are at the net, the distance the racquet must be moved to make a volley is much less than that required to make a ground stroke. Since you will thus have time to protect yourself with the racquet, you are probably as safe at the net as you are in the backcourt.

Beyond that are the dividends to be gained from volleying at the net. Assuming that you have the shots, the ease of winning points is directly proportional to your proximity to the net. The ball comes to you above the net. The closer you are to the net, the more court on the other side is opened to you as a target. With each step that you retreat toward the baseline, you increase the area that you must cover and diminish your target area.

But really, the best way to cure your fear of the net is simply to force yourself to come to net. It might be helpful, from a psychological point of view, to schedule some matches with weaker players who don't hit the ball too hard and to come to the net in these matches much more than you normally do. Then, as you begin to gain some confidence, try it gradually with your regular partners. Start conservatively, coming to net only on those shots which your opponent cannot hit back with any power. If you are diligent about this practice, you'll soon be playing a more aggressive net game in doubles.

Chapter 12 Strategic Serving

The Strategy of the Serve
by Bob Harman

Wouldn't you think that every tennis player with a spoonful of brains would serve accurately? The serve is the one shot in tennis that is never stroked on the fly or on the run. It can be hit from the same stance, at the same distance from the net and with the ball at the same place in the air. It can be practiced alone and at leisure.

Any average player certainly should possess a reliable, accurate serve. There is no reason why everyone who plays frequently should not be able to put his first serve into the deeper part of the service court, with fair speed, 65 percent or more of the time. Yet we all know how few players do that.

You don't need strength or perfect coordination to be a good server. You simply need a little wisdom and a bit of tactical knowledge.

Notice that I did not say that everybody should be able to *blaze the ball past the opponent*. If this is what you try to do with most of your first serves, maybe this is why you seldom get them into play. Serving too hard is a common mistake among club players. It destroys accuracy.

Some players tell themselves, "I don't mind missing my first serve so often because when it goes in I usually win the point." Yet these are the very players who lose more games than they win simply because of those missed first serves. That's the crucial fact they never face.

What it comes down to is percentages. What does it profit a player to hit seven faults for every ace? Wouldn't it be better to serve with less speed but more accuracy? Isn't a steady server likely to win more points than the spectacular but erratic type who gambles on all-or-nothing serves?

Most points in tennis are scored on errors, even at Wimbledon and Forest Hills. A consistent serve at moderate speed can draw many errors from opponents if it is aimed toward weak spots. Some of the great champions—Ken Rosewall and Fred Perry come immediately to mind—never served thunderbolts; they just put their first serve where they wanted it, and that alone gave them an edge. They beat many hard servers whose first serve too often was a fault.

How about you? Are you one of the unhappy souls who serve too many faults? If so, let's consider how you can make more strategic use of your serve.

Instead of whacking your first serve as hard as you can, experiment with using slightly less force. Slowing your serve by 10 percent may increase its accuracy 35 percent. Find out just how hard you can hit the ball and get it in. Let this amount of force be your limit most of the time. Promise yourself to stop gambling on your serve. Smooth it down to a precision weapon, a rapier instead of a sledgehammer.

Once you can control your serve, you can concentrate on putting it where it bothers your opponent the most. Usually that is the backhand corner. Few club players have a strong backhand return of service.

As your opponent is forced into errors or weak returns off his backhand, he will begin edging leftward to take your serves on his

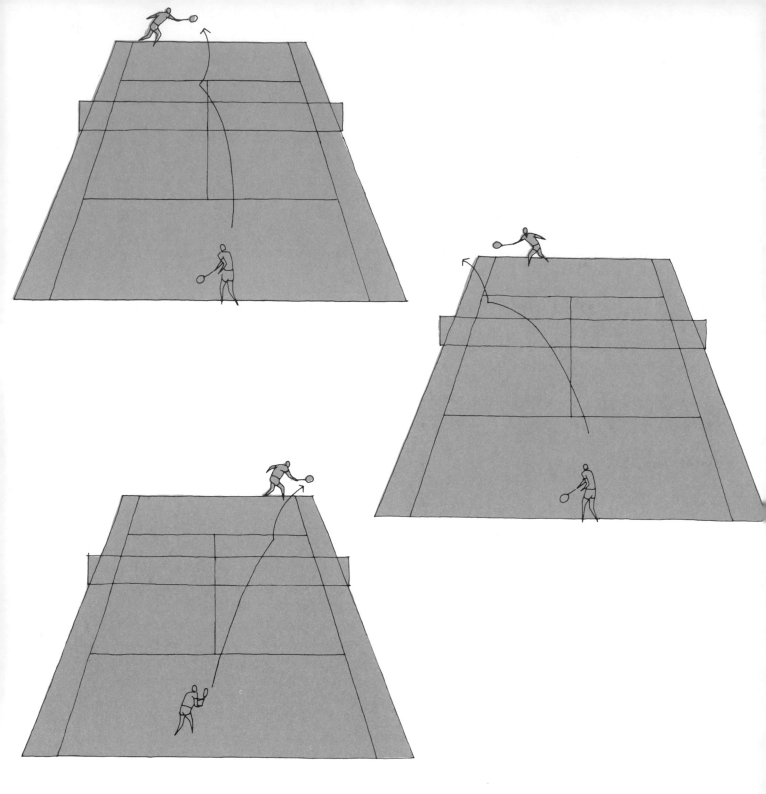

It pays to keep your opponent guessing when you serve. If he has a weak backhand, then serve to that side (top left). Should he begin to anticipate your serve by moving over to the center, then slice a serve to his forehand side (above). The sliced serve will break away and pull your opponent far out of court. If you are playing a good ground stroker, you'll find it pays to stay back against his returns but try an occasional feint toward the net just to keep him confused (left).

forehand. That is your cue to switch to a different serve for a while.

Variations on the Serving Theme

There are other ways of using your serve strategically than simply probing your opponent's weakness with it. One way is to vary it: flat one time, slice the next. If you can vary your serve and disguise it (which you can do by using a backhand grip), you enjoy the same advantage as a baseball pitcher who can keep hitters off balance with an assortment of pitches. Sometimes you can win points on your serve by hitting the ball directly at your opponent. This is especially true when he is standing within the baseline. Instead of trying to hit the corners in this situation, just aim for his belt buckle. Because he is so close, he has less time to decide whether to use a backhand or a forehand when the ball arrives at his belt buckle (or at his knees).

If he moves too far back, use the slice. Your serve will break away to his forehand and he will have to run farther out of court to return it.

Some receivers like a fast serve. They are geared to smack it back fast, even when you send it accurately to their backhand. Your best strategy against such formidable opponents is to slice the serve with as much spin as possible. This slower serve and trickier bounce upsets their rhythm. When they get used to the slice, break their timing again by mixing in your faster flat serve.

If your opponent has powerful ground strokes, don't rush the net behind your serve or you'll get passed. To keep him worried, you can follow your serve into the forecourt two or three times per set on those occasions when you've made an especially sharp serve. Feint a rush every now and then. But when you feint, stay far enough back to take his return on the bounce. From the backcourt, you can comfortably concentrate on making him run from corner to corner.

The Second Serve

Now for that feeble second serve. Beef it up. It should be fast enough that you don't have to go onto the defensive as soon as you've hit it. Instead of those marshmallows you've been sending over because you're afraid of double-faulting, use the slice service I've just recommended.

If you develop a reasonably fast second serve, it will strengthen your game in two different ways. On your first serve, you will be less tense and worried because you will no longer dread the thought of your second serve. Conversely, your opponent won't get the psychological lift that usually comes when he sees the first serve go harmlessly past him. With no cream puff to look forward to, receivers are less confident and aggressive.

Don't feel humiliated by the lack of a murderous first serve. The only players who consistently get a big serve into court are those who can practice it for hours at a time. Your serve is still your main offensive weapon despite a lack of blazing speed. An accurate serve will win more points than a red-hot but erratic one. If you win most service games, you will seldom be beaten.

What to Do When Your Serve Goes Sour
by Vic Braden

The serve is the only shot in tennis on which you get two chances, and yet how often do you flub both of them? How many times do your knees turn to jelly when you are down match point and you miss your first serve?

I'm willing to bet that you don't really know what you are doing wrong. You probably excuse yourself by saying that you are having an off day. Wrong. You can fix your own serve when it goes sour. Below are listed common problems of faulty serving and the suggested cure for each.

Problem: My serve is too long.
Cure: Toss the ball a little farther in front of your body. It helps to think "forward" as you toss and "upward and out" as you hit.

Problem: I feel completely uncoordinated.
Cure: Get the rhythm back into your serve by counting "1-2-3-4" like a dance instructor as you swing. Take it easy and don't rush your serve.

Problem: My serves go into the net.
Cure: Keep your eyes and chin up. Fasten your eyes on the ball at all times. Keeping your chin up will prevent a slouching posture that will pull down your hitting arm and the ball.

Problem: I've lost my confidence.
Cure: Have a friend verify your errors by charting your serves (see above). Find the precise area of error and then go away and practice hitting targets to rebuild your confidence.

Problem: I get angry as my serve worsens.
Cure: Focus your attention more closely on the ball. Try to transfer your emotions to the ball—that's your only opponent in the serve.

Chapter 13 Overhead Strategy

The Strategy of the Smash
by Alex Mayer

The basic strategy of the overhead isn't very subtle at all. Its purpose is to win the point then and there. There are two ways of doing this. One is through power. The other is through accuracy and consistency. For the average player, I recommend the latter strategy.

Placing the Ball

It is often said that if you don't have a good serve you won't have a good overhead. I do not agree. If you can simply place the ball with your overhead, you will win as many points as you would by thundering the ball across the net. Placement is basically a matter of upper-body position. Notice I said "upper." The proper ready position for the overhead is sideways to the net. From this position, you can place the ball anywhere on the court without moving your feet. You simply turn your upper body slightly just before impact. By turning the upper part of your body, you avoid telegraphing the stroke, which is what occurs if you turn your feet in the direction in which you want to hit the ball.

The Overhead in Doubles

The placement rules for overheads differ in singles and doubles. In singles, the rule is to hit the ball where your opponent isn't. In doubles, you are generally better off hitting overheads down the center in between the two opponents. Of course, if your opponent is silly enough to be close to the net when you hit the overhead, by all means aim right at his feet. This shot is virtually unreturnable. On the other hand, I think it is generally bad tennis to aim your smashes directly at your opponent. It's simply not proper etiquette, even if he has miffed you in some way.

On the Bounce or the Fly?

On many lobs, you have a choice between hitting the ball on the fly and hitting it on the bounce. I recommend hitting overheads on the fly whenever possible, for two reasons. First, you are going for a winner, and so the less time your opponent has to get into position, the better your chances. Secondly, the falling ball is coming at you with more velocity, and frequently all you have to do is deflect it in the right direction to win the point.

The Elements and the Overhead

There is one exception to the rule I've just stated. It's in playing outdoors on a very sunny or windy day. Sun and wind are obstacles to the efficient execution of the overhead, so it sometimes pays to let the ball bounce first. If the sun bothers you during the warm-ups, you should experiment a bit by turning to the right or left to see which direction gives you less trouble. If the wind is

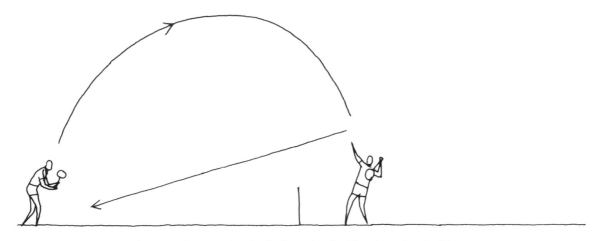

With a short lob near the net, always take the ball on the fly. The dropping ball has quite a high velocity, so that all you have to do is deflect it in the right direction, often with a short punching stroke.

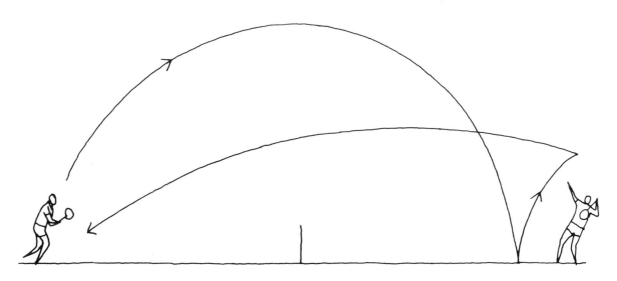

With a deep lob close to the baseline, let the ball bounce and try to return the shot as deep into the opposite court as possible. It's better to hit a neutral deep shot than to hit a fast overhead that lands in your opponent's service court, where it can often be put away easily.

gusty, it is generally a good rule to let the ball bounce, since it's difficult to line up an overhead properly when a ball wavers on its descent.

Playing the Deep Lob

Inevitably, there will be times when a lob lands so close to the baseline that you are forced to the back fence. Some players insist on smashing back this shot, but I advise against it. Even the strongest overhead, hit that deep, is probably going to land in the service court and give your opponent an easy chance for a putaway. The strategy here should be to lob as deep as possible. You will have plenty of time to show off your overhead muscle on shorter lobs.

In singles, try to place an overhead out of your opponent's reach. If you hit it on the fly, your opponent is less likely to have enough time to reach the ball and you will therefore increase your chances of winning the point outright.

Don't Let the Overhead Psych You

by Allen Fox, Ph.D.

Every player, from beginner to the most experienced tournament pro, has felt frustration after missing an easy overhead. There is, in fact, more "psych" connected with the overhead than there is with any other stroke in the game. Among the professional players, it is known to be a "confidence" shot and is the first stroke to go when you lose your touch or become nervous.

Most strokes are hit as an immediate reaction to your opponent's shot. There is a smooth interaction between his stroke and your reply. But the lob hangs in the air and you must wait for it, giving you time to think, to initiate action and to worry. Your shot is no longer a reaction; its success or failure appears to be entirely *your* responsibility. This "challenge" aspect of the overhead causes tension.

Because overheads look easy, they are laden with potential embarrassment. Note the expectant hush that falls over a group of onlookers when a player moves under a high lob. They all remember the times they have hit the ball into the fence on the fly, or hit it off the wood and over the fence, or, worse, swung ferociously and missed the ball completely. Other than tripping over the net on a victory jump, nothing is more humiliating than whiffing an overhead.

Not only must a player cope with the mechanics of the shot; he must also cope with his ego and a possible snicker or two from the sidelines.

The question is, what can you do about it?

First, don't assume that an overhead is an easy shot, or that it *must* be put away with the first smash. This notion leads to the two cardinal sins of overhead execution: (1) rushing the stroke and (2) trying to hit the ball too hard. Either of these misjudgments will cause you to miss many short, low lobs that actually are setups.

Second, do not "think" at all while hitting the shot. This rule goes for any shot in tennis, but because there is so much time and so much ego involved with the overhead, there is a greater tendency here to start thinking. That makes you vulnerable to fear, which destroys timing and slows reactions.

The usual result of thinking during the overhead stroke is to let the ball drop too low, duck your head slightly, take your eye off the ball and mis-hit the shot. A typical symptom is feeling rushed at the crucial moment, even though you have had plenty of time to prepare for the stroke. If you start thinking, you will never have "enough" time, no matter how much time you have.

The answer is to develop a patterned set of movements and thoughts. Learn through practice what is reasonable, optimum power for you and use it on all overheads. Everyone is different, so you needn't try to hit the ball as hard as Stan Smith—even on the easy, short ones. Just hit them solidly and you will get your share of winners. I believe that if you have been having problems hitting overheads, you are probably trying to hit the ball too hard. By doing that, you sacrifice consistency and add to your feelings of uncertainty about the stroke. Knowing how hard to hit the overhead eliminates one item to think about during the stroke.

Don't try to outguess your opponent on where to hit the ball. Just pick a side, keep your eye on the ball, relax and hit the ball. Don't change your mind during the stroke.

If your opponent anticipates well and returns your overhead, more than likely his shot will be weak. He won't have time to hit a hard passing shot unless he is particularly strong or lucky. If he lobs again, repeat the same pattern at the same pace. Resist any temptation to watch him or to rush your stroke. He will eventually guess wrong.

The basic countermeasure to the feeling of nervousness which may accompany any stroke is to develop a smooth pattern of movements and thoughts which will fill your mind and block out random and destructive thinking.

Since the overhead has so much emotion associated with it, mental discipline must be exercised if you want to hit the stroke effectively.

Chapter 14 Lobbing Strategy

How the Lob Can Lift Your Game
by Bob Harman

In discussing the strategic aspects of the lob, I can do no better than to cite the wisdom of that wily, likable basketball star and coach, Bill Russell. Russell used to talk about writing a master's thesis on psyching the opposition, and his first law applies as well to tennis as to basketball. "Make the other player do what you want him to do," Russell always said. "Get him to start thinking. If he is thinking instead of playing, he is yours."

What does this have to do with the lob? Everything. One of the great values of the lob is that it can be used to great strategic advantage against different types of players. We have discussed the mechanics of the lob (page 105), and hopefully, you now understand how to hit offensive and defensive lobs with equal facility. Effectiveness in both cases depends on deception and ability to place the ball. If you can angle lobs cross-court to the far corner, particularly to the backhand corner, you possess a formidable weapon indeed.

The Value of the Lob

One extremely valuable aspect of the lobbing game is that it keeps your opponent on his guard. The mere threat of a lob gives you a better chance to successfully execute a passing shot. In singles, even more so than doubles, this threat discourages your opponent from camping on top of the net, just waiting to cut off any passing shot you attempt.

Get your opponent to respect your lob. You'll find him backpedaling much of the time in anticipation of it, and this is when your passing shots become noticeably more effective.

After the Lob

Much of your effectiveness in using the lob is a matter of what you do after hitting it. Your strategy depends largely on your opponent. You can usually tell early in a match how he reacts to lobs: whether he smashes them deep or angles them or patty-cakes them across the net. Once you understand his pattern, you can anticipate better.

If your opponent is not too quick and the lob you put up goes over his head, it is a good idea to come to net. Only the top pros have the ability to scramble behind a lob and hit the ball back with any power.

Then again, if your opponent has a weak overhead but still persists in coming to net, you needn't worry much about returns—just lob him to death. Even if he has a super overhead, it does not mean you should abandon lob psychology. Send some lobs up anyway just to keep him guessing. Soon he will begin to wonder, as he approaches net, just what you're going to do: pass him, lob deep or lob high? He may also start to wonder, on a very hot day, whether he can continue scrambling back for deep lobs.

Once you get him thinking this way, he is, as Bill Russell might say, "yours forever," and you can wear him like a bauble on a charm bracelet.

The offensive lob.
Hit from inside the baseline, it is a low, quick shot designed to win a point by catching the opponent off guard.

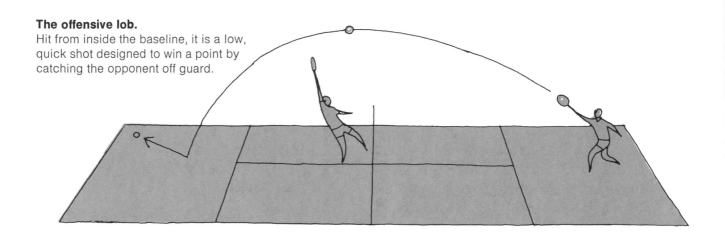

The defensive lob.
Made from deep in the court, it is hit high in order to give the player time to recover his position.

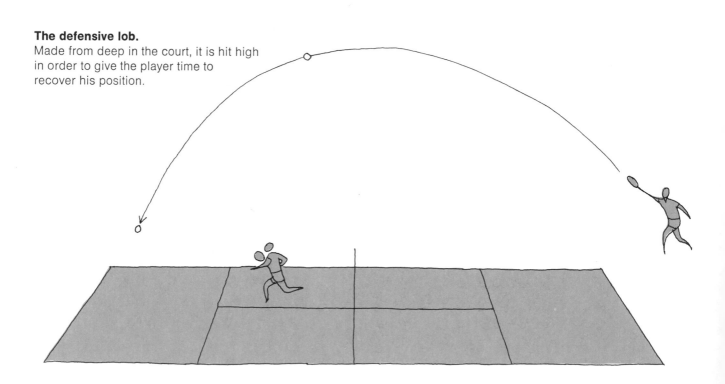

The Professional Approach to the Lob
by John Alexander

Before the advent of open tennis, professional players tended to be pretty condescending about the amateur game. One reason for this was that amateurs, in general, neglected to use one of the most important shots in tennis—the lob. The lack of a lob, in fact, explains why some outstanding amateurs have had trouble through the years when they first joined the professionals. The pros always try to play percentage tennis—to play each point in the manner that best ensures eventual success. The lob is a vital element in percentage tennis.

One example of how a top pro plays the percentages with the lob is the way Ken Rosewall employed it to upset Stan Smith in a World Cup match at Hartford, Connecticut. Early in the match, Rosewall would launch a quick, low offensive lob whenever he had an opportunity for what normally would have been a passing shot. This tactic upset Smith's rhythm and forced him to stay farther back from the net than he usually does. With this opening, Rosewall then began to use his passing shots and went on to a decisive victory. Here the lob was intended not so much to win points as to open up the court for Rosewall's passing shots.

Percentage tennis is probably most important when a player is in the receiving court, and this is where the value of the lob really comes into its own. The receiver's first job, of course, is to return successfully as many serves as possible. If he does that and if the server charges to the net, the receiver on his second shot will often be presented with the opportunity for a passing shot. Should he take it?

There are a number of factors to consider. The better the shot your opponent has made, the less chance you have of countering with a successful passing shot. And if you are forced to make this shot from wide in the court, your chances of running down any return by your opponent are slim indeed.

In this situation, a high, defensive lob might be just what is called for. First of all, it is a shot that almost anyone can execute nine times out of ten. Secondly, it is a slow shot that has a long way to travel, giving you a much better chance to recover your position. There are also subtler advantages. Putting up lobs regularly for your opponent to smash can wear him down. Also, when a player's best volleys are consistently retrieved and returned as lobs that he has to smash, he will probably feel a need to make his volleys a little bit better. That means his errors will increase.

In addition to the two basic kinds of lobs, the offensive and defensive, there is a variation that fascinates many fans: the topspin lob. I'm quite often asked why I don't use it, and my answer usually is that Rosewall doesn't, and therefore it obviously doesn't pay.

The truth is that the topspin lob doesn't fit in with percentage tennis. It is a very difficult

Contemporary players with outstanding lobs are
Billie Jean King (below), Rod Laver (right) and Marty
Riessen (below right). Laver is one of the few
practitioners of the topspin lob.

shot to bring off and generally can be made only off a relatively easy shot. Two players, however, have been consistently successful with the topspin lob: Rod Laver and Ilie Nastase, who can hit it off either the forehand or the backhand.

Marty Riessen is another good lobber, and he has made the shot a big part of his game because he has to. He scrambles around to retrieve wide balls that many other players would not bother trying to get. Since it often puts him badly out of position on court, he resorts to the lob to give him time to recover.

Jimmy Connors uses the shot effectively, and disguises it fantastically. Because he has a two-handed grip, he does not have to take the racquet back very far in order to generate the power needed to lift the ball. That makes it hard for an opponent to tell when his lob is coming, so he uses the shot as an offensive stroke to catch the opposition off guard.

Some good lobbers actually use the shot to cover up a weakness. John Newcombe, for example, lobs a great deal off the backhand because he lacks a good passing shot from that side.

Smith and Arthur Ashe, on the other hand, lob very little, and that represents, I feel, a flaw in their games. Smith lobs only when he is in extreme trouble. This defect hasn't seemed to hold him back, but I think he'd be even better if he learned to lob more. Ashe's infrequent use of the lob has, I believe, stopped him from beating the top players consistently. It means that he does not have an alternative play to the passing shot. Consequently, his opponents can come close to the net and not worry about the lob.

In using the lob, the average player should remember that not all points have equal value. Imagine, for instance, two situations in which you are the receiver. In one situation, the score is 40–0; in the other, 30–40. In each case, your opponent volleys deep and wide to your backhand. Since the shot opportunity is the same in both situations, you might think the lob would be the best shot in both cases, and it is. However, why waste this—your best play—when the score is 40–0 and you are in a near-hopeless situation? Why not save it for a more important occasion, such as when the score is 30–40? Your shot then will be less likely to be anticipated by your opponent because you haven't already played it in a similar situation.

Don't look upon the lob as the perfect answer every time you are in trouble. There is no such shot in tennis. For any shot to be effective, there has to be an element of surprise. The lob is an invaluable weapon when used with discretion, but disastrous when played poorly or too frequently.

Chapter 15 Drop-shot Strategy

Get the Drop on Your Opponent

by Doris Hart

The drop shot is one of the most underrated and underutilized strokes in present-day tennis. I've always made heavy use of it because I like its element of surprise. The drop shot can be disguised so well that your opponent is kept guessing right up to the last second. Besides, a mixture of drop shots and lobs will force your adversary to run up to the net and then rush back to the baseline. This tactic eventually wears out even the toughest players. Drop shots are especially effective in women's tennis, inasmuch as very few women move as well toward the net and back as they do from side to side.

Perhaps the most important strategic value of the drop shot is that it disrupts the steady baseliner. Some of today's young players, especially the girls, can stand at the baseline and rally all day. A well-executed drop shot will bring a baseliner scrambling to the net, making him or her vulnerable to a good passing shot or a deep lob.

Unfortunately, few of today's juniors take the time to learn the touch that is needed for the drop shot. That's why we see those long and, to my mind, boring rallies. The drop shot was one of the earliest strokes I added to my repertoire after establishing the basic ground strokes. I saw the value of a shot that would destroy my opponent's stroking rhythm.

When to "Drop"

Strategically, the best time to employ a drop shot is when your opponent is on the baseline and hits a ball that bounces short inside your service line. A weak second service is a good example. Since many players do not rush the net after serving, you can generally drop-shot a weak second serve with ease. Unlike many other situations that call for the use of the drop shot, in this one it's often a winner, particularly if you put enough backspin on the stroke.

Almost any situation in which the opposing player is badly out of position is ideal for a drop shot. With a baseliner, you often can angle a ground stroke to force your opponent to run out of the court. Most likely the return will be weak and can be dropped crosscourt or down the line as a clean winner. Setting up this kind of situation can be tough if you are up against a good scrambler like Billie Jean King or Rosie Casals. Against the average club player, however, you should have no difficulty, since he will not be able to regain position quickly enough after the shot.

Whenever you decide to drop-shot, don't hang back. Always follow the shot up to the net. Chances are your opponent, if he gets to the ball, will drop-shot right back to you and you'll have to be close to the net in order to return it at all. The better your drop shot, the closer to the net you can afford to go. If your shot is only fair, then I suggest that you stay at about the service line. If you see that your shot is going to drop very close to the net, then go close to the net yourself. In either case, try to volley any ball returned off your drop shot. That way, you stand a good chance of passing your opponent—who will, most

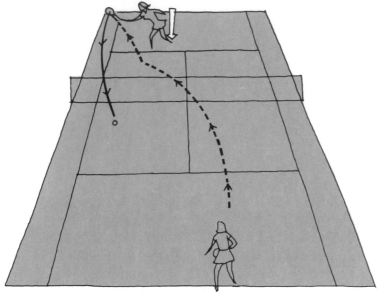

If an opponent (near court) has a weak second serve and does not rush the net, that presents an excellent opportunity to angle a drop shot for a perfect winner.

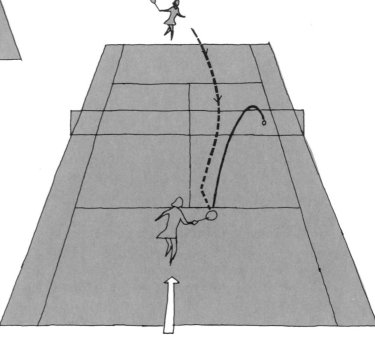

When a steady, ground-stroking opponent insists on staying back at the baseline (far court), use a drop shot to bring her scrambling toward the net. A passing shot or a deep lob then figures to win the point.

Any time an opponent (far court) gets out of position so that she makes a poor return, take the opportunity to angle a drop shot that she will not be able to reach.

likely, be close to the net unless his anticipation has been very good.

Don't worry too much about your ability to drop-shot effectively. Even a bad drop shot will cause your opponent to run around, and in the long run, that will tire him.

In my matches, I'd often start out with drop shots which weren't working very well. Later on in the match, my drop shots would improve. At the same time, my opponent would generally be tiring and not making quite the same effort to get to them. As a result, a good number of those drop shots became winners.

One fallacy I'd like to dispel is that you can drop-shot only from around the midcourt position near the service line. If you have practiced the drop shot sufficiently, you should be able to drop-shot from the baseline, particularly off a medium-pace ball. That is where the element of surprise really counts, because your opponent will not expect you to try the shot from that position. If you do it successfully, you can keep your opponent guessing for the rest of the match.

Another common fallacy is that the drop shot cannot be used in the doubles game. While that is often true in men's tennis, it certainly is not the case in women's tennis, in which the server rarely rushes the net. The drop shot can be used in doubles if both opponents stay back or if one or both of them have a relatively weak service. In these instances, angle it toward the server to force him to run

up to the net. Even if you are faced with a team that rushes to the net, you can use a modified drop shot, one that drops at the feet of the opposition. That tactic is especially effective on grass, where the ball will not bounce very high.

Facing the Drop Shotter

When facing a drop shotter, you have to anticipate the chances of the shot's being used and be prepared to move forward to return the shot. If the opposing player does not move in, the best tactic is to drop-shot right back—particularly on grass or clay courts, where the ball will not bounce high—for an easy return. Use plenty of angle if you can, because that will make your opponent run farther. If your adversary does come to the net, then I would recommend a lob to force him back to the baseline and set him up for yet another drop shot.

I can't emphasize enough the need to learn the drop shot as early as you can and to practice it as frequently as possible. Have someone go out onto the court with you and feed you medium-pace shots at both service line and baseline. Try to build your confidence, especially with angled drop shots. Learn to use this underrated shot and see how easily it can demoralize your opponent.

Exploit Your Drop Shot
by Allen Fox, Ph.D.

The drop shot is, by and large, a losing proposition in itself. But the *threat* of the drop shot is something else again. It is probably the truest psychological stroke, since most of its value comes not from its capability of winning points, but from its psychological impact on your opponent.

The threat of the drop shot instills fear and discomfort in your opponent's mind, and anything that makes your opponent uncomfortable can't be all bad. It can annoy, frustrate and humiliate him. It forces him to play a step or two closer to the net, leaving him vulnerable to the deep drive. It breaks up his rhythm, because he anticipates having to scramble to the net at any moment.

Finally, it makes him think, and thinking during a point disrupts and disintegrates the learned reflex patterns that are basic to fluid ground strokes.

The drop shot is an accessory stroke. One could become a top tournament player and never hit a drop shot. Marty Mulligan, one of the finest European clay-court players, never hits drop shots. He just pounds ground strokes. So does Jan Kodeš. That is because an effective drop shot must be hit in reply to a weak or short ground stroke, preferably from inside the baseline. Mulligan and Kodeš take such opportunities to attack with their ground strokes, often advancing to the net.

Although players who use the drop shot excessively do not generally fare well, there is one exception: Whitney Reed. Reed was a wild character who was ranked No. 1 in the United States in 1961. He thrived on drop shots, hitting them at every opportunity and from any position on the court. When Reed was hot, his opponent was in for a maddening afternoon, in addition to a good beating.

I met Reed for the first time on just such a day in the semifinals of the National Intercollegiates in 1960. Much to the amusement of the spectators, he jerked me around the court like a puppet. When the giggles started, I became so flustered and embarrassed that I lost all concentration. My main goal was to get off the court as soon as possible. [Editors' note: The author won the Intercollegiate title the next year.]

But because of his excessive reliance on the drop shot, Reed was not a consistent winner. In the finals of the Intercollegiates, he played Larry Nagler, a quick former basketball player who was really not in Reed's class at that time. Reed's touch was less than golden on this day, and Nagler doggedly chased every weird shot that was thrown at him, finally outlasting Reed in five sets.

So it is with anyone who is too dependent on drop shots to win points. You should drop-shot only enough to threaten your opponent—not so much as to cost you too many points.

Do not drop-shot on crucial points. In rare instances you might have the touch to pull it off, but you may mistake wishful thinking for touch. You are likely to be nervous on big points, and attempting a drop shot when you are nervous is very foolish.

Finally, fight any inclination to drop-shot when your opponent has command of the point. If you are being run from side to side, you sometimes get the insane urge to try a desperation drop shot to extricate yourself and turn the point around with one master-stroke. That almost never works. Drop-shot only when you are in control, you have confidence and the point is expendable.

Ready to spring into a service return, professional Charles Pasarell plans his strategy to put the server on the defense.

Chapter 16 Return-of-service Strategy

The Best Ways to Improve Your Service Return
by Bob Harman

The object of all tennis strategy is to gain the offensive and keep it—to place the ball so adroitly that your opponents can't do much with it.

Each point begins with the server on the offensive. He has all the time he needs to hit his serve, with full power and dead aim if he is good enough. But what then?

When you're receiving, can you risk the offensive from the server? Quite often you can, if you have a good plan in mind.

Planning before the server hits the ball is important. In the fraction of a second while it zips toward you, there is no time to figure out various moves you might make. Most players get sloppy on returning service because they just hit it on impulse, with no particular plan in mind. With that attitude, they kick away their first, and probably best, chance to put the server on the defense. A poor return is usually a lost point.

On the other hand, a crafty return means that the server loses the edge. The instant the ball is returned to him the scales can be almost balanced, ready to tilt either way.

As you read this, consider the strategies available to you in returning service. Knowing your game and your opponent will help you prepare what to do.

Assuming that the server is in your own class for speed and accuracy, you will want to alter your tactics slightly depending on whether the game is men's or women's singles or doubles or mixed doubles. Let's consider each situation in turn.

Men's Singles

It is folly to try to whack back a first serve for a sure winner. If the server does not rush the net, plan to drive your return deep to his backhand, except in the rare cases in which his backhand happens to be his stronger side. Play it safe. He hopes his serve will force you into an error, but it needn't if you have decided that you will aim at least six feet inside the corner, with no more speed than you can be sure of controlling. The besetting sin of receivers is trying to return the serve too hard.

If he does come in behind his serve, don't try to pass him unless you are a real expert. Try for a shallow shot that will just clear the net, landing low on his backhand or forehand. It is the last thing he wants.

Every time his first serve misses, you should move up inside the baseline. This bothers him. He knows you are in position to take the offensive unless his second serve is especially good.

If he rushes the net behind his second serve, just welcome him with a low, shallow shot. After a few games, his tongue will be hanging out.

Women's Singles

Except in world-class singles competition, a woman is unlikely to take the net behind her serve—and even there, only a few of the top-ranking players do so almost invariably.

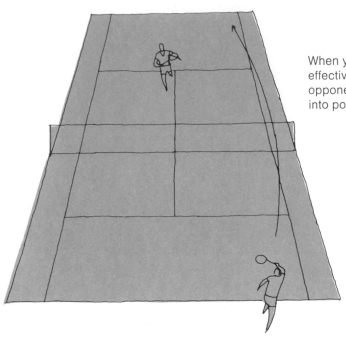

When you're returning serve in singles play, one effective ploy can be to stroke a forehand deep to the opponent's backhand. Then move diagonally forward into position to volley.

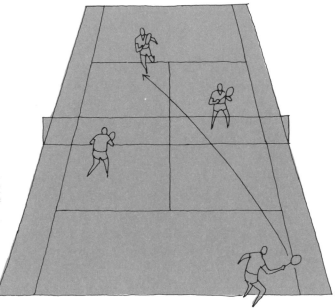

When returning serve in doubles, try to send a forehand drive crosscourt—aiming usually to get it low and shallow so that it will land at the feet of the server if he's coming to the net.

It is too exhausting. So fix the thought firmly in mind that you will return serve with a deep drive to the backhand. Then follow it in or not as you wish.

Study your opponent. Does she really hate to come into the forecourt? Then make her do just that by feeding her short shots. You will have a good chance of passing her with your second shot, or of lobbing over her head.

On her second serve, you should be in closer and be planning to return it harder, into one corner or the other. Just be sure not to

beat yourself by hitting too hard and knocking the ball out of court.

Doubles

Almost invariably, you should plan to hit your return crosscourt, so that the server must handle it, rather than the player at the net. You know the server will be coming in, so your shot should be low and shallow, forcing him to volley up. If you're clever, you can angle it into the alley and pull him far out of court. You want to force him to send back a rising ball, which you or your partner at the net can jump on. If the server's partner keeps poaching on your return—leaping across to intercept your low crosscourt shot in the forecourt—you have three options. You should decide in advance which you'll try:

(1) You can hit your crosscourt shot harder, hoping he can't get to it. This is the riskiest and most difficult of your choices. (2) You can hit down the line instead of crosscourt. This is suicide if the net man isn't poaching, but a certain winner if you catch him going the wrong way. (3) You can try a quick lob over his head.

As you get ready to receive the second serve, key yourself to move on it quickly, so that both you and your partner will be at the net. Often you can do this on the first serve, but it is essential on the second if you want to win.

Mixed Doubles

If this is a sociable game, the men won't be trying to use male strength to knock the racquet from a woman opponent's hand. But if it is a competitive match, most shots will be to the woman—or the man if he's the weaker player. If you are a man receiving a man's serve, try to pass the woman at the net at every opportunity. If you are a man receiving a woman's serve, always return it low and shallow.

If you are a woman receiving a woman's serve, expect the man at the net to poach on your return. Make up your mind in advance either to angle the return too wide for him to reach or to catch him off balance with a shot down his alley or a quick lob over his head.

If you are a woman having trouble with a man's serve, try to lob over the woman's head. His second serve will usually be moderate enough so that you can plan to chip crosscourt, or use the lob.

All this sounds complicated because I've covered quite a number of different situations. But in any given match, you will encounter only one or two of these. So you shouldn't have any trouble selecting your strategies in advance.

The general rules are rather simple: In doubles, the best return of serve is usually low and crosscourt. In singles, the best return is deep to the backhand or forehand—whichever is the weaker side—unless the server rushes the net; in that case, return low and shallow to either side. Adjust this strategy as you find your opponent's strengths and weaknesses, and you will break service surprisingly often.

The value of tactical skill in doubles is aptly illustrated by the success of John Newcombe and Tony Roche, one of the finest doubles teams in the world.

Chapter 17 Doubles Strategy

The Tactics of Doubles
by Bob Harman

The mental aspects of tennis assume more significance in doubles than in singles. Consequently, and happily, you do not necessarily have to play harder to improve. You simply have to play smarter. Playing smarter involves fixing certain principles firmly in your mind. Oddly enough, the best time to review these principles is not *before* you play, but *after*. You don't get much time during a match to think about what you're doing right or wrong. Afterward, though, when you have the time to isolate your mistakes, you can think about them so that the next time you play you'll hear a warning bell when you're about to make the same blunder.

The Postgame Self-interview

Let's set up a hypothetical situation. You have just finished playing what you are sure has been the worst doubles of your life, and you're taking a shower. If I were to construct a stream-of-consciousness debriefing, it might run like this:

What did I do wrong today? Nothing went well from the minute I stepped on court. We had only an hour to play, as usual, so instead of the fifteen minutes I really need to warm up, we rallied only five minutes, and I could feel my bones creak.

Could I have used those five minutes better? Instead of hurrying to work the kinks out of my stroke, instead of trying to exercise my-

self into a glow of tigerishness, maybe I could have concentrated on the two essentials:
1. Keeping my eye on the ball. (Like most players, I often look away.)
2. Hitting through the ball so that it feels good against my racquet on every stroke.

O.K. Next time I'll spend the five minutes tuning up my Eye and Feel.

Checking Out the Serve

Now, how about the game I served? First, was I serving from the best place—far over toward the sideline? Or did I absentmindedly serve from near the center line, as everyone does in singles?

Second, was I hitting my first serves too hard? Getting them in is vital in doubles. Better remind myself next time that smart doubles players use an arching serve that kicks wide or a slicing serve so that they have more time to move forward and be in position before the receiver can return the ball. And how about my second serves? Too gentle? Every time they were, both my opponents grabbed the net position.

Third, was I aiming every serve toward the receiver's forehand? Guess I forgot that the usual intent of the doubles serve should be to force the opponent to receive on his backhand (unless he happens to have a superstrong backhand or a forehand so punk that I

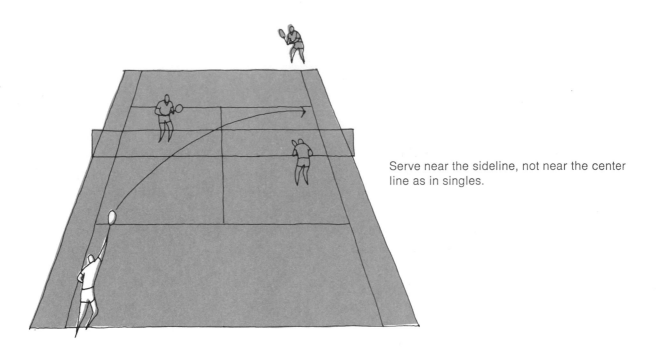

Serve near the sideline, not near the center line as in singles.

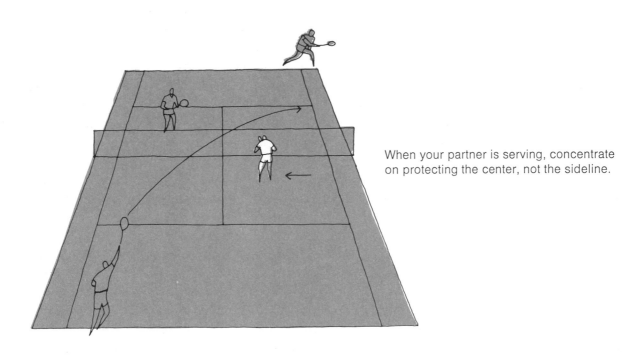

When your partner is serving, concentrate on protecting the center, not the sideline.

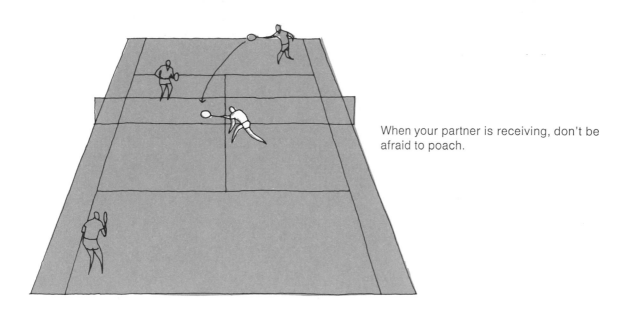

When your partner is receiving, don't be afraid to poach.

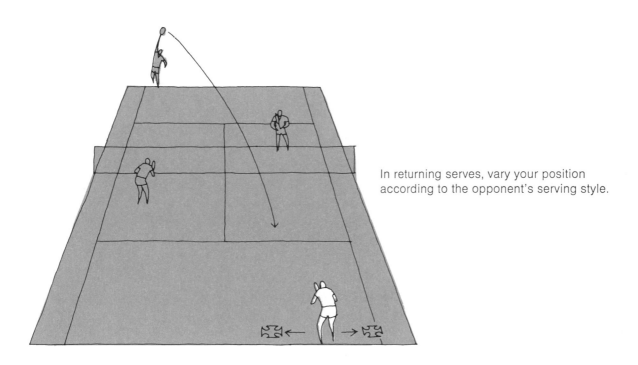

In returning serves, vary your position according to the opponent's serving style.

ought to make him return all serves with it).

Fourth, what did I do the instant after I hit my first serve? Did I start forward? Or did I stand craning my neck to see whether the ball went in? I know I should reach the net at least two or three times in each of my service games, even if I'm not a sharp volleyer, because I'll never improve if I don't. When I'm not rushing, I should move up a few feet inside the baseline anyhow after my serve.

Returning Serve

When I was returning service, did I stand where I should? The average player stands in the same spot against all servers—and I know this is dumb. Next time I'll study each server for a few games and see where his serve usually lands, then edge over to be in a good position for it. And I'll break myself of the habit of waiting behind the baseline to receive.

After all, this isn't singles, so I'm not trying to return service with a deep drive to the baseline (which the net man can intercept easily). I'm just trying to get my racquet onto the serve and make the return a low, shallow crosscourt shot. Crosscourt is the name of the game in doubles.

What about returning second serves, which are bound to be weaker? Did I get ready by moving up even closer? And did I remember not to try to murder them, because that gave the net man a waist-high ball to angle back at my sideline?

And that pretzel backhand of mine. Did I make the mistake of overprotecting it by playing far to the left? I've got to try more of my weak shots to develop an all-court game. Which reminds me: I must lob more. The average doubles player is a sucker for a lob; he crowds the net too closely.

What did I do when my partner was receiving a serve? Did I just stand to the side like a two-legged millstone? Probably I was out of too many plays that I could have influenced. Sure, I know the safest thing to do is to do nothing, and stay away from the net as if it were electrified, but where's the challenge in always being conservative?

I hereby resolve that when my partner receives, I'll mosey up just inside the service line. When it appears he'll have trouble with the ball, I'll hustle back on the defensive, ready to retrieve that volley which is sure to come when a receiver makes a weak return. But if he's making a good return, I'll move up to do some volleying myself.

I won't be afraid to poach a little when I can cut off a shot at the net by stretching. My partner won't give me the acid eyeball if I win the point, which I'm likely to do with that kind of shot. And when I don't plan to poach, I'll pretend to anyway. A little swing and head feinting, not overdone, can keep you alert and be worrisome to your opponents.

That covers three of the four positions. How about the fourth? Was I playing smart when my partner was serving? I know I should be in the center of the service court, about halfway between the net and the service line.

But I also know that I have a silly habit of edging over toward my own alley, just because that big space on the outside makes me nervous. I've got to remember not to do that. Few players try the difficult shots down the alley, and I can easily block them if they do, even from the center of the service court.

So I'll quit hanging around the alley. And when my partner has served, I'll edge over to the inside, where most of the action is. If my opponents never lob, I'll close in on the net whenever my partner sends the ball skimming low over the net.

If they lob, I'll still stay close whenever my partner doesn't have to run too far for the ball, because he'll be smashing it and I should pounce on their return. On deep lobs, I'll retreat, and if my partner has to switch sides to retrieve the shots, I'll cross over too. No more standing rooted to the ground and leaving half our court unguarded.

That's about everything, isn't it? Almost.

In general, was I sending balls too high across the net, where they could easily be volleyed back? Did I keep my own volleys deep, but soft, so that they didn't bounce high? Did I remember to hit the ball at an opponent's feet whenever I could? Was I caught in the backcourt when I should have been taking advantage of a good shot by moving up? Was I trying too many straight shots down the line instead of hitting the diagonal crosscourt one that is harder to cut off?

That's a lot of questions. Too many to assimilate in one postmortem, probably.

But you should keep asking them. One by one, match by match, you'll learn to avoid more of your old mistakes. Playing brainy tennis is a matter of habit. Get the habit!

The Doubles Touch
by Ron Holmberg

In singles, a player can sometimes get away with a slashing attack—going for winners all the time by hitting a big serve and hard ground strokes. But except on those relatively rare days when his game is "on," this type of player frequently has trouble playing doubles. Even then, it doesn't make for an enjoyable game—especially at the club level.

The point is that doubles warrants a different approach than singles: an approach that emphasizes "touch"—a sense of being able to feel the ball on the racquet. The reason is that in doubles it is placement more than power that wins points. Hitting powerful ground strokes deep into the corners may be sound strategy for singles, but in doubles those same shots are often easy pickings for the net man.

Let's cite some examples of how touch succeeds in doubles where power doesn't. You are receiving serve and you find that the net man is knocking off your returns for winners. Here is a chance for the most underrated shot in doubles—the lob. Lob it high and, most of all, deep. Force your opponents back so that your team can take command of the net.

Now let's look at touch from the server's point of view. You've been serving and following in your serve, but your opponent has been coming in behind his return. Normally, in doubles, you want to hit your first volley hard and deep, but in this case, with your opponent closing in on the net, it's better to hit a soft, low volley; this shot will force him to hit up, giving your side an excellent chance for a putaway.

When all four players are at the net, you should always use a softer shot to keep the ball low and at your opponents' feet. The idea at the net is to maneuver the ball and keep it low so that your opponent will hit up and give you the easy volley. When your opponent's shot comes in high, hit the ball hard down the middle for a winner.

In tennis, as in any other sport, the ability of the offense to do a variety of things is what keeps the defense guessing. Therefore, a steady diet of either hard shots or soft shots is not as effective as a combination of the two. One thing to remember when you try to produce a soft shot at your opponent's feet is that it is usually easier to hit the shot crosscourt, because this allows you a greater distance to hit the ball. That is not quite as delicate as a soft shot hit straight ahead. Secondly, the crosscourt shot in doubles is usually the percentage shot, since the net man should be able to handle most straight shots.

Use all these softer shots. You will enjoy the game more, and you may suddenly find yourself a very popular doubles partner.

Receiver's Tactics

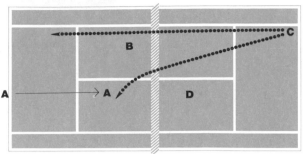

1. The player returning serve (C) should direct the ball at the feet of the server (A). For variety, though, he should sometimes fire a return down the line to keep the net man (B) honest.

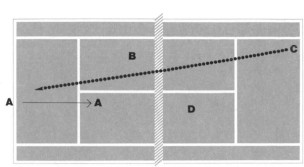

2. The other time to stroke the ball hard in returning a serve (C) is on those occasions when you're aiming it down the middle of the court between the two opponents (A and B).

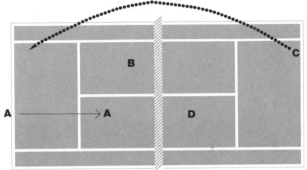

3. The most underrated shot in doubles is the lob. The player lofting the ball (C) should make sure it is sent high and deep to pull the opponents (A and B) away from the net.

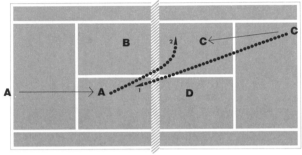

4. When the player returning serve (C) attempts to come in behind his shot, the server's (A) best countermove is a low, soft volley laid in smartly at the opponent's feet.

Server's Tactics

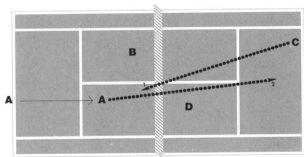

5. The server (A) should hit his first volley hard and deep only on two occasions. The first is when the opponent (C) is staying back near the baseline after his return.

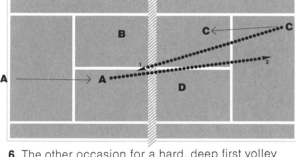

6. The other occasion for a hard, deep first volley by the server (A) arises when he is going for a winner by hitting between opponents (C and D) who are at the net.

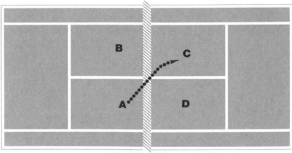

7. With all four players at the net, the idea is for the player (A) to stroke the ball softly and keep it low so that the opponent (C) will hit it up.

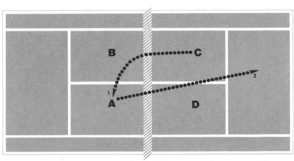

8. When a shot comes in high in up-close net play, that's the time for the player (A) to move in for the kill by hitting hard down the middle between the two opponents (C and D).

Margaret Court and Marty Riessen have won the U.S. Open mixed-doubles titles three times.

Mixed Doubles: The Women's View
by Margaret Court

The biggest problem women face when playing mixed doubles is psychological. They approach playing with men with a defeatist attitude, assuming that they are at an athletic disadvantage on the court even though, in many cases, they play better than their male partners and opponents.

When a woman has this sort of attitude, it shows up in her game. Seeing herself as a helpless interloper, either she tends to hold back with the idea of hurting her side as little as possible (while her partner handles everything), or she tries to overcompensate for her supposed inadequacies by straining to be too helpful and by taking on more than her capabilities allow.

Now, it is true that men tend to be stronger, more mobile and more experienced in sports than women, but this is not to say that a woman can't hold her own in a match. Even though men generally hit harder than women, power is not always the winning factor in doubles. And as long as a woman doesn't panic when a ball is hit hard at her by her male opponent, she can deal with the power shot quite easily—not by trying to wallop the ball back just as hard, but by standing up to the ball, to block it or chip it back.

Nothing to Fear but Fear

Some women seem to be particularly reluctant to go to the net in mixed doubles, even though they play the net fearlessly against women players who often hit harder than men. Here again, the problem is psychological—a question of fear. But it's a fear you must overcome if you are to truly enjoy mixed doubles. For if mixed doubles is to have any meaning, the man and woman must work as true partners.

Which brings me to an important point. Since doubles of any variety involves teamwork, it helps immeasurably if you have a partner whom you like both on court and off. I have been very fortunate in the partners I've played with in major tournaments: Ken Fletcher of Australia and Marty Riessen of the United States.

Fletch was an amusing, irrepressible sort who always knew how to keep me relaxed. He used some of the most outrageous language you've ever heard on court, and he'd always apologize profusely. Or during a critical point in a match, he'd gesture toward the stands and say, "Look at that bird in the fifth row. What do you think of her?"

Marty is more serious during a match, but he talks a lot with me about what we should or shouldn't be doing. He's also a thoroughgoing gentleman. Even though he was eliminated early from the men's events at the 1972 U.S. Open, he stayed around for more than a week to play the mixed doubles (which we won). Not many men would do that.

Honesty Pays

Congenial as partners can be, you still have to work together well on the court. Establishing a good relationship with a new partner begins, I think, with honesty right from the start. I feel a woman should confess whatever weaknesses she may have right at the beginning of a match. That way, the man can adjust. Don't wait until you have flubbed your eighth straight volley before admitting that the shot gives you trouble.

By and large, it seems to work best if the woman lets the man act as team captain—especially since he is usually the better player and usually has the bigger ego. The man should make most of the decisions, such as who serves first. But in no sense should the woman be a junior partner.

Dividing Responsibility

Generally speaking, it is sound strategy to let the man take the most difficult shots in a mixed-doubles match (assuming, of course, that he is the better player). Chances are, the man will be able to do something more with a difficult shot than you can. This is one of the things I like about mixed doubles. In women's doubles, you and your partner are usually equal in ability, so the question of who handles the tougher shots can sometimes pose a problem. Not so in mixed doubles. Since the man is generally stronger, the team should always take advantage of this by having the man take the toughies.

Still, you must not leave too much to the man. Take the shots that are clearly yours. If you hesitate, you will make more errors, and confusion will reign on your side of the net. When the opposition lobs to your side of the court, for instance, have a go at it. If you defer to the man, he will be badly out of position for the next shot.

What should you do when the opposition concentrates its fire on you? One of the basic tenets of mixed-doubles strategy calls for a team to pick on the other woman because she is usually the player more vulnerable to attack.

When this happens, I enjoy it. I welcome the challenge, and I always tell Marty or Fletch or whomever I'm playing with to do the same thing to our opponents. If you don't direct your attack at the woman, especially in tournament play, you are surrendering points. The woman shouldn't mind; the fact that she's out there means she wants to play, and she should be prepared to take her chances.

If you are the object of this kind of assault, there is only one thing to do: try to keep the ball in play until your partner gets a chance at it or can move in to intercept it.

The lob is a good stroke to fall back on when you get into trouble in mixed doubles. It is particularly useful against the other woman when her partner is serving and you are having trouble getting the ball back.

Mixing Tennis and Marriage

When you select a partner for a mixed-doubles tournament, I would urge you not to choose your husband. There have been very few successful husband-wife teams. It is similar to married partners in bridge; it usually doesn't work.

One reason is that husbands and wives tend to take out their feelings on each other when things go wrong on the court. If the husband is the better player, he tends to get impatient. She then tends to sulk, and before you know it, a marital squabble is in full cry.

If you want to be on court with your husband, play on opposing teams. There are seldom any fights in that situation.

Regardless of who your partner is, don't make extravagant apologies for errors you commit. A simple "sorry" will suffice. Then forget about it and get on with the next point.

Play the best you can. Don't get uptight. Above all, remember that the object of mixed doubles is to get some exercise, have fun and, if possible, use the opportunity to improve your game.

Mixed Doubles: The Men's View
by Marty Riessen

When a man goes on court for a mixed-doubles match, there is one fundamental question he has to answer right away: should he fire every ball he can directly at the woman on the other team? Winning logic says yes. Chances are, she is the weaker player, and if you are out there to win you should try to take advantage of her inadequacies. Yet all those old strictures about gallantry and fair play say no. It just doesn't seem gentlemanly to embarrass or humiliate a woman simply to win a tennis match.

After I started playing mixed doubles on the tournament circuit, it took me some time to resolve the question. I simply could not bring myself to hit all-out against the other woman. I was finally persuaded to do so by Margaret Court, my regular partner now in professional mixed doubles. She would say, "Come on, Marty, hit it at her. She can take it. You're not going to hurt her. If we want to win, you've got to do it." My wife tells me the same thing when we play socially. She even gets angry when I fail to play to the other woman. "Don't be so nice," she'll say. "Let her have it."

I think that what a man decides to do should hinge largely on what is at stake. If it is strictly a social game, there is little satisfaction to be gained and possibly a friendship to be lost by showing up the woman. The idea in social mixed doubles should be for all four players to have a good time, get a chance to use all their shots and try to improve their game. Winning in these circumstances should be entirely secondary, and the man should give the other woman a break by placing the ball so that she can hit it. If she can't hit it, she can't improve.

But in tournament or other serious play—whether at your local courts or at Forest Hills—the man should have no compunction whatsoever about playing to the other woman, assuming she represents the weak point on the opposing team. She should expect it. It is not a real contest if you fail to give it your best effort.

Establishing Communication

Before you square off in a mixed-doubles match, it is important to establish what your partner's capabilities are. Not everybody is lucky enough to have a Margaret Court for a regular partner, as I do.

It pays off before a match to go over such things as each partner's strengths and weaknesses (assuming you haven't played together before), which of you will handle shots hit down the middle and whatever you know about the talents of the opposition. Margaret and I usually have a short briefing before a big match. She'll remind me about certain traits of the other woman (e.g., Billie Jean King likes to serve to the forehand on grass), and I'll do the same with the other man (e.g., Owen Davidson likes to use a lot of topspin on his forehands). Your briefing doesn't have to be as refined as that, but informed comments of any kind will help.

It seems to work best if the man assumes unspoken command of the partnership. Margaret seems to want me to do that and always defers to me on the key decisions. Like any good partner, male or female, she also always suggests, never criticizes. This kind of rapport is essential to success. I once played with Billie Jean as a partner and all she did was boss me around. I haven't played with her since.

Winning Tactics

Once the match begins, who should serve first? Often the man will be polite and let the woman start out first. That is a mistake. The man is almost always the stronger server and more likely to win; he should go first.

There are two possible exceptions. If the woman would wind up serving directly into a bright sun by going second, it may be best to let her serve first. If there is a stiff wind blowing the length of the court, it could be a good idea to let her serve with the wind to add speed to her delivery.

When the man serves, he should never ease up in his delivery to the woman. It is vital that he win those games, at least in a serious match. To lose them is like walking the pitcher in baseball.

Often, you'll want to overpower the woman by using your hardest delivery. But I've found that women do not have all that much trouble returning a fast ball. What gives them problems is serves that make them move. They seem to have difficulty going after balls with a lot of action on them, balls which they have to chase. So I generally use a slice serve, which veers away from an opponent, or a

kick (twist) serve that bounces high and changes direction.

In almost all cases, the man should play the backhand court—again, assuming he is the stronger partner. There have been some successful exceptions to this rule. Rosemary Casals and Ilie Nastase won Wimbledon in 1970 and 1972 with Rosemary playing the ad court. And Stephanie DeFina Johnson and I teamed together well with Stephanie in the ad court. She was a left-hander and was quite comfortable in what for her, of course, was the forehand court.

Even if the woman is left-handed, it is generally preferable for the man to be positioned in the ad court. That is where the close games are decided one way or the other, and that is where you want your strength.

The man is usually expected to cover more of the court and take more balls, especially the tough ones. It means he may have to poach a little bit more than normal without being downright hoggish about it. Be sure that your partner is agreeable to these tactics, and in purely social games be careful not to take on too much of the load, because it can irritate the other players.

In serious mixed doubles, the lob is an important element of strategy. Most women cannot handle lobs as well as men. They do not move back as easily for them and, when they do reach them, cannot smash them as hard. A man had better be ready to cover lobs from the opposing team because the chances are they are going to be lobbing him too.

When you go back for a lob on the woman's side, she should always cross over to protect the side of the court you have vacated. Urge your partner to do that—but don't be too insistent about it. I remember one match during the 1967 French Championships when Tom Okker of the Netherlands was playing with Virginia Wade of Britain and kept yelling at her in vain to cross over. Finally on one point he hollered, "Get over there," and she was so petrified she ran completely off the court.

That's hardly what you'd call teamwork. In the end, your success in mixed doubles will really depend on teamwork, which is the essence of any effective doubles play.

It is crucial that you give your partner support. Encourage her, never carp at her. For example, if Margaret is having trouble with her serve, I don't snarl at her. I will make a suggestion, such as aiming the ball down the middle a bit more. Or if my game is off, she may gently mention that I am playing too fast. We each know the other is doing everything possible to win, so on-court lectures are not required.

It helps that we are friends off the court. I think you will be both happier and more successful in mixed doubles if you pick a partner you get along with and enjoy as a person.

Many men, including some of the touring pros, seem to feel that mixed doubles is a waste of time. I disagree. I find it good fun. When played professionally, it offers a lot of spectator appeal because it is fairly novel and much of the public plays doubles or mixed doubles. It can produce some very good tennis as well.

The average man should not look upon mixed doubles as a second-class brand of tennis. Recognize it for what it is: different, to be sure, but interesting and rewarding in its own way.

Stan Smith angles a volley out of the reach of Australian
Syd Ball as his partner, Bob Lutz, watches in the
ready position in case Ball achieves a miracle return.

Doubles on the Pro Circuit
by John Alexander

The best professional doubles team, to my mind, consists of two players who have never achieved top ranking in singles—Fred McMillan, who uses two hands for most ground strokes, and colorful Bob Hewitt, who uses any means available to intimidate opponents and officials.

There is nothing unusual about two so-so singles players teaming up as a topflight doubles team. Success in doubles rests in a grasp of tactics and an almost intuitive knowledge of your partner's moves. McMillan and Hewitt, who won the Wimbledon doubles and the national doubles titles of South Africa, Italy and Germany in 1967 before turning pro, have a real feeling for each other's reactions. Each knows when his net man will intercept returns of serve and when the receiver will cross over to cut off a volley. They play so well as a doubles combination that they won the 1974 WCT doubles championship, decisively defeating John Newcombe and Owen Davidson in the finals match.

Two fine singles players, on the other hand, may prove a less-than-ideal doubles team. When Bob Lutz and Arthur Ashe, two excellent singles players, for example, tried to make it as a doubles team, it simply didn't work, and I think the trouble was Arthur.

Ashe doesn't seem to give much thought to intercepting service returns or following up his own returns—carry-over, I think, from his singles tactics. He frequently goes for outstanding shots that in singles are often winners and require no follow-up. But in doubles, with two players to cover the court, he often gets caught out of position when these super shots are returned.

So if you are not the best singles player in your league, you still have a chance for some satisfying wins and perhaps a trophy or two by specializing in doubles. There is no need to be awed by the singles winners as long as you and your partner understand doubles strategy and work well together.

Among the top pro doubles players, perhaps the best record is owned by Roy Emerson, who has a knack for picking good partners—in particular, Rod Laver. Fans who only occasionally have a chance to watch Emerson and Laver in action probably consider Laver the dominant player. But this is far from the case. Emerson makes most of the constructive moves. Taking full advantage of Rod's great service returns, Roy places tremendous pressure on the incoming volleyer, who never knows if Emerson will go across, stay, or fake a cross then double back.

Marty Riessen and Tom Okker represent another example of an outstanding doubles player (Riessen) teamed with a performer of incredible talent (Okker). Riessen's doubles play is very similar to Emerson's. He makes a lot of interceptions and invariably follows in his service returns. One of Riessen's favorite ploys is to cross over when Tom has made a weak return. This often creates indecision in the mind of the player with the easy volley, causing him to miss the volley completely or to play it so safely that Marty can volley it back to save a point that otherwise would have been lost.

The combination of Riessen's shrewd tactics with Okker's ferocious topspin forehand makes it difficult for their opponents to win their own service games and extremely difficult to break serve against them. Probably the best chance to break through against Okker-Riessen is on Tom's serve when he fails to get the first one in consistently. His second ball is not severe enough to force the receiver onto the defensive or create openings for Marty's net play.

Stan Smith and Bob Lutz utilize their natural strengths to good advantage as a team. Lutz takes full advantage of Smith's powerful serve to win many points with his first volley. Smith uses his height to cut off many first volleys after Bob's return of serve. They play a straightforward game, simply doing most things well.

Allan Stone and Nikki Pilić create chances for service breaks by forcing their opponents to hit to their strengths or play risky volleys. Pilić is known for his vicious forehand. After Pilić returns serve, Stone simply moves toward the center of the court, forcing the incoming volleyer to try for his sideline or else volley to the Pilic forehand.

Players who succeed in doubles, whether in the pro ranks or at club-level play, know that doubles is not won with isolated great shots. It is a game of strategy. Two players who work well together can often defeat opponents invincible in singles play.

Chapter 18 General Strategy

How to Chart Your Game Plan

by John Alexander

In tennis, as in most other sports, winning depends not only on how well you perform but also on how well you tailor your tactics and overall approach to your opponent. Most players in the pro ranks know the strengths and weaknesses of other pro players and will go over these factors in their minds before a match. I know I do, and I think that the average player, assuming he knows his opponent, can do the same. Here are some of the basic questions you should be asking.

1. What shots is he capable of hitting? In first observing a player we are aware of how he hits his shots. The idea is to look for *faults* in stroke production. This is where we will find his weaknesses. Some common faults are:

a) Failure to change grips for the backhand shot, thereby making an offensive backhand more difficult to produce.

b) Late backswing, making the shot rushed, resulting in loss of accuracy and power.

c) Failure to get down to the ball—which makes the sighting of the ball guesswork (all-time great Lew Hoad often said if he had eyes in his stomach, he would never miss a shot) and restricts following through the flight of the ball.

2. What sort of shape is he in? Naturally, all tournament players are very fit, but because of their age or their own natural shape they can have some physical limitations. Two examples would be John Newcombe and Tom Okker, who are both very fit men, yet very different.

Okker is extremely quick. Because of his lightness, however, he lacks power on service smash and high midcourt volleys, and is possibly more vulnerable to fatigue in long matches on hot days. Newcombe, on the other hand, lacks the speed of Okker but has the height and strength for powerful overhead shots and more stamina on court. It's a rare day when he loses in the fifth set.

We can say, therefore, that a player's physical makeup and condition can govern to some degree not only his style of play but also his vulnerable shots.

3. What is his mental approach? I think that more matches are won and lost upstairs than with a good forehand and a lousy backhand. For instance, some players can lose a match in the first few games because of their inability to pull themselves together when they are behind. On the other hand, there are players who often give away the first set if it isn't going too well, trying to lull you into a false sense of security, then deliver 100 percent early in the next set, hoping to upset your rhythm and gain an early break. Some players who have poor strokes yet do exceptionally well rely heavily on such tactics, and one must be aware of the dangers of such players when confronted with them.

There are really no strict rules that govern the performance of all tennis players. Where we find faults we may not always find weaknesses. Examples: Tom Okker's forehand, which he hits off his right foot without bending, with a late backswing and with excessive topspin, and Ken Rosewall's backhand, which he can't even topspin, are two of the greatest single shots in tennis today!

Vic Seixas is a former Davis Cup star and U.S. and Wimbledon champion.

How to Play
Catch-up Tennis
by Vic Seixas

One of the oldest and most useful tennis axioms is that you should always change a losing game. This axiom is the key to playing catch-up tennis.

If you find yourself in a catch-up situation, there are several ways you can go about changing your game. Let's say that you have been playing an offensive brand of tennis, hitting hard and rushing the net. But your opponent has been passing you, using lobs adroitly and generally outmaneuvering you. How do you deal with this situation? The answer should be obvious. Adopt a more defensive approach. Vary your game a little more. Stay back, keep the ball in play and give your opponent more opportunities to make errors.

On the other hand, let's say you've been playing conservatively but it isn't working. The advice here is to reverse the process: adopt a more aggressive style of play.

Changing Placements and Speed

Apart from changing your basic style of game in a losing situation, you can also change the kind of placements you've been making. If you have been going down the middle, for instance, you might try directing the ball out to the side more often. Or if you have been concentrating on your opponent's backhand without result, switch to the forehand.

Another effective way of changing a losing game is to vary the speed on the ball. An opponent can get grooved returning balls hit at the same velocity all the time, so it is a good idea to mix fast with slow balls and some with a fair amount of spin on them. This will throw off his timing.

Never Give Up

In a losing situation, your attitude is crucial. To make a successful comeback, you cannot afford to lose poise. I first learned this at Forest Hills in 1940 when, on my 17th birthday, I was paired against Frank Kovacs in an early round. Kovacs then ranked No. 2 in the United States (behind Riggs), and there was no way I was going to beat him. Yet I won the first two sets 8–6 and 7–5. Word quickly spread of a big upset in the making, and a large crowd soon gathered around our court.

But Kovacs, to his credit, did not panic. He realized he was up against a young player whose game was hot and that it would cool off sooner or later. That's exactly what happened. I started out playing with abandon, figuring I had nothing much to lose. When I got ahead, it occurred to me I might actually win. Suddenly, it all got to me; I became unnerved—and Kovacs nailed down the final three sets 6–4, 6–4, 6–2.

It was a lesson I recalled some years later when I was placed in Kovacs' position in the 1952 Davis Cup Interzone Finals between the United States and Italy. My first match in the singles was against Fausto Gardini. He was a fine player, but I felt I was better. He opened up with some fantastic tennis, and there was little I could do about it. As he waltzed off with the first two sets, I told myself all I could do was stay with him until he came back to his normal level of play. He did, and I pulled out the match in five sets.

Of course, it is much better if a player can jump out ahead, so that he isn't forced to come from behind. To try to do that, my approach to a match is usually to play it safe at the start—sort of like a boxer feeling out his opponent in the first round or two. I don't attempt to blitz him by swinging from the heels. My goal is just to keep the ball in play for the first few games and to concentrate on avoiding any errors. It's not that I poop the ball—I just play with a certain margin of safety. That way I get a line on the type of game my opponent is playing. More important, he is the one who is likely to start making errors. Once he does, he will often get nervous and the pressure will mount on him, forcing still more errors.

If a player is compelled to play catch-up, it is vital that he be in good shape and know how to pace himself through a match. If he expends a lot of energy in the early stages, it will hurt his chances later on—especially if he's an older player. Or if he goes all out in a fourth set and loses, he may be in trouble in a fifth set. So a player should be prepared when he appears on court to go the distance, and he should learn how to spread his energies over that period without hurting his game.

To me, stamina is one of the most telling elements in any sport. That is why I find fault with some of the tie breakers that have been introduced into tennis. They reduce the importance of physical conditioning by putting a time limit on a match; in effect, they penalize the player who is in the better shape. If a tie breaker is to be used, I prefer the type that is deferred until a final deciding set, as is the practice now at Wimbledon.

Stamina has, obviously, played a role in most great comeback matches; but one that particularly comes to mind is the thrilling duel in the 1953 Davis Cup Challenge Round between Tony Trabert of the United States and Lew Hoad of Australia. In fact, this match was a grueling, seesaw affair that involved spectacular comebacks by both players. Hoad had to win if Australia was to retain the Cup.

It began under gray skies in Melbourne with a long, bitterly contested first set that Hoad finally won 13–11. He went on to take the second set 6–3, and Trabert's chances looked fairly hopeless. Then it started to drizzle. The balls got heavy. This didn't bother Trabert. Hoad, however, did seem to mind, and he began missing. Trabert captured the next two sets 6–2, 6–3, and the momentum seemed all in his favor.

Indeed, a Trabert victory seemed inevitable as the fifth set progressed, because Hoad was having great difficulty holding his serve. Still, it had gotten to 5–5 when Hoad went crashing face first across the wet sideline in vain pursuit of a volley. The partisan crowd gasped, and Hoad lay there looking grim and spent. At that point, Australian coach Harry Hopman reached over and tossed a towel in

Hoad's face. Hopman's reputation for tactical wizardry was such that the gesture was interpreted by the press as a sign of monumental genius. Whatever it was, it had a dramatic impact on the match. The crowd laughed, Hoad grinned, the tension evaporated and the Australian rallied to save the set, the match and the Cup by the score of 7–5. (I should add that Ken Rosewall completed the successful Australian defense by beating me in four sets the next day.)

Most of the time, of course, comebacks don't work for the simple reason that the other player is ahead because he's better. So changing a losing game may not make any difference. But there are times, as we've seen, when it is possible to play catch-up tennis successfully.

Tony Trabert (far court) and Lew Hoad, opponents in an epic 1953 Davis Cup match. Note that, as often happens in net situations like this, Hoad has not had time either to change his forehand grip to the backhand or to hit from the traditional backhand stance.

Guide to Gamesmanship
by Fred Perry

Tennis matches are to be won. Tactics, fitness, stroke ability, adaptability, experience and sportsmanship all are necessary. So too is "gamesmanship." Particularly when you are the underdog in a match. I have seen it turn the trick more than once. Sometimes even the opponent wasn't aware of it—and the spectators certainly hadn't a clue. But it was there.

The ABC's of Gamesmanship

Gamesmanship begins with knowing your opponent. You should know what the opponent likes and dislikes, what he can do and what he can't. You should know his mannerisms, how he reacts under tension, when he is nervous and how it affects his game.

During my competitive career, my opponents were well known to me. I had studied them. My object was to force my game on them and make them play the way I wanted. I never worried about what they could do on a court. All that interested me was what they *couldn't* do. That was what I intended to give them. I knew that provided I was able to do what I planned with the ball, there were only certain things they could do in return. The problem arises when your opponent is able to force you to do what *he* wants.

The number-one rule of gamesmanship is this: never give your opponent the chance to play his own game. If he likes wide balls, make sure they come close. If he prefers them close, be sure they are wide. If he plays fast, you must slow down and waste time. If he's slow, you speed him up. Should he need high bounces to make his best shots, feed him with low stuff . . . and vice versa.

Some players are most dangerous when they can get set before making a shot. Keep these players on the move all the time. If they are volleyers, take the net position away from them. If they are baseliners (as most Europeans usually are), bring them in to the net. The basic rhythm of opponents must be broken up as much as possible.

On service, some players prefer to have their opponent ready and in position to receive before they go through the serving action. All their rhythm is geared to that ritual. Go along with it, but at a critical moment— say, the middle of the set and a chance of a break in serve—don't be there at all. It doesn't have to be too obvious, either. You can have mistaken the score and be on the wrong side to receive. Or a shoelace can have come untied. It won't be noticed, but it might do the trick.

Perry was the first player to win all of the four major international championships.

Ilie Nastase's court antics have not always endeared him to fellow players, but he is acknowledged, for better or worse, to be the supreme "gamesman" in tennis.

Some play in silence and need it to concentrate. Give them plenty of noise and conversation. Others prefer a word or two—so, in that case, not a sound comes from you. I have seen players deliberately string a towel up under the umpire's chair just so that they wouldn't have to listen to the remarks from an opponent when changing sides.

Volleyers in particular are helped by crowd reaction. Their game is spectacular and they need to have the crowd behind them. An opponent has to make an extraordinary shot to get recognition, and if he does, the chances are the public will then be watching him. To get them back, the volleyer (if he knows his gamesmanship) will come up with something to draw attention his way.

It could be an apparent injury, an argument with a linesman, an untied shoelace or, better still, a fly in the eye.

This last bit of histrionics, of course, calls for a lengthy drama of going over to a convenient linesman and having him take a look. The main thing, though, is to get the crowd looking at the volleyer while the other poor fellow, who has just made the shot of his life, will be standing out there like a bump on a log.

It always helps to know that the spectators are watching you. If they are and you make a lucky shot off the wood or get a netcord, they will applaud automatically because you've won the point.

Putting Gamesmanship to Work

There is more to this game than meets the eye. Servers always show new balls to the receiver. Most spectators believe this is merely a courtesy. It could be—but it could also be to point out to the receiver in no uncertain terms that the server has the new balls—a distinct advantage to the power boys of the game.

Gamesmanship can be used in many ways. For instance, if you have a sore spot or blister on one foot, there is a problem of pushing off on that foot. Limp on the other foot and you are likely to fool your opponent into playing right into your hands by attacking on the side that doesn't affect your footwork.

Most players have a wonderful array of shots on the practice court, but will use only those they have confidence in and know they can make when it comes to a match. Try everything a few times right at the start, when it doesn't really matter one way or the other as far as actual points are concerned. Let the other fellow think you can and will make a particular shot; you know you can't, but he might think you can and play away from it.

If you like your tennis and enjoy a spectator's role, look for some of these ploys the next time you attend a big match. It may help you understand just what really goes on underneath, especially when the going gets rough.

If you play a club-level brand of tennis, you can have a lot of fun employing a bit of gamesmanship—especially when you're the underdog and there's really not all that much to lose. But be prudent about it: you can lose friends if you make your gamesmanship too obvious.

Watch for it when you are a spectator, but watch it carefully if you try it yourself.

Adjust Your Game to Indoor Play
by Butch Buchholz

The explosive growth of indoor tennis is presenting players of every caliber with yet another element of the game to conquer: the transition from outdoor to indoor play.

The adjustment can be a problem even for professional players, as I found out during my debut as a rookie on the pro circuit back in 1961. My first month on the tour was extremely frustrating. We were in New Zealand. One day we'd play outdoors on clay in Christchurch; the next day indoors on wood in Hamilton; the next day outdoors again, but this time on grass, and so on. I was so put off by the changes that I lost the first six matches out of the nine I played on that tour. Rod Laver, too, had problems adapting his game to indoor conditions when he turned professional in 1963. The lights were a major problem for him.

In those days we all had difficulties playing in indoor arenas that were not specifically designed for tennis. But now, of course, the average indoor club is built specifically for tennis.

Indoor play offers the kind of consistent conditions that simply do not occur outdoors in most parts of the country. There are no sudden gusts of wind to raise clouds of blinding dust or cause the ball to veer out of court; no dazzling sunlight; no high humidity (assuming that the indoor club is air-conditioned, as many newer clubs are). Conditions in some indoor clubs are so perfect for the average tennis player that you may find that you do not look forward to making the transition to outdoor play at the end of the indoor season.

Tennis lighting is improving, so that this problem is disappearing, but if you play indoors in a facility that utilizes direct lighting, you may have to modify your game slightly. For example, to avoid looking directly into bright overhead lights when serving, you may have to alter your toss and usual service position. Sometimes it means moving over toward the center line when you're serving for doubles. Other times, a slight shift of the toss to the right or left is all that is needed. To find the solution to this problem, experiment with your serve. You should be able to find a

The limited space between indoor courts can result in game interruptions as balls stray across from adjoining courts or as neighboring players charge after sharply angled shots. It's best in such cases to agree to call a let.

To avoid distractions from overhead lights when you're serving indoors (left) it may be necessary to alter the toss or the service position. A really high lob (right) may hit the ceiling above the court. If it does, the player loses the point.

comfortable position during your warm-up serves.

The lights can also pose a problem when you hit an overhead smash, particularly if the lights are directly over the center of the court. The only solution here is to move back as quickly as possible for the lob so that you have plenty of time to position yourself without having to look into a light fixture as you smash.

These lighting problems should eventually disappear as more sophisticated systems are developed and installed to replace the older lights.

Watch the Lob

You also must accustom yourself to the limited space around an indoor court, both in terms of the distance between courts and in terms of the height of the ceiling.

When I'm out of position in a match, my instinctive reaction is to toss up a really high lob to give me time to recover my position. When I'm playing indoors, I sometimes forget that I have only 35 to 40 feet to work with and, sure enough, I hit the ceiling. Nothing is more frustrating than to think that you have hit a good lob and then to have the ceiling return the ball rather sharply and lose the point. It doesn't happen too often, but it is very annoying to lose the point that way.

Restricted Space

Many clubs now use nets to divide their courts. Nets stop most of the stray balls from adjoining courts. But they can pose a slight hazard of their own, namely, that of running into the net and getting entangled like some hapless fish. Very often I have gone wide to chase a crosscourt shot or a sharply angled volley and found myself bounding into the net.

There is little you can do about the restricted space. Just be cautious in going for wide shots, and also be careful about running back for shots that go over your head. Even if the court has a canvas backdrop, it may be located close to the wood or steel frame of the building. Running into a steel girder can be most painful; you can break a racquet or a limb.

In the interest of sportsmanship, it is best not to use the space limitations as an offensive weapon. Don't try for the angled shot in order to get your opponent to run into the net. You'll be unpopular and it just isn't good tennis.

Because indoor tennis is quite expensive, indoor players try to squeeze as much tennis as possible into their sessions. Unfortunately, this often means beginning a set before there has been time to warm up sufficiently. This enthusiasm is commendable, but it can prove costly. It takes only one extra effort on an early serve or smash to develop a sore shoulder that can last for months in the winter. It is wiser to get to the court early and take the extra time to warm up properly. If the club has no facilities in which you can warm up, do so when you go out onto the court. It may seem that you are wasting valuable time, but it is better in the long run. Similarly, do not rush outside when your game is over. Take a shower, change and cool off properly before leaving.

PART III

Practice and Conditioning

Chapter 19 Practice

Drills for Drill-haters
by Paul R. Siemon

Your tennis game has certain weaknesses you know you should try to correct, but you don't like to drill and you can concentrate only when you play. Besides, you have only a few hours a week in which to play and you do not want to waste time. There is a solution to this dilemma: to combine drills with playing. You can continue playing sets and playing to win. Simply vary the scoring method in such a way as to emphasize your weaknesses. Here are some suggestions:

1. For Better Ground Strokes

If you have a tendency to net ground strokes, two variations can help. One way is to play a normal game except that any ground stroke hit into the net loses the game, regardless of the score. For better players, charge a game lost to any ground stroke hit within the service box. Both scoring methods will force you to hit your ground strokes higher and therefore deeper.

2. For Better Volleys

If you don't volley enough, set up a situation in which any missed ground stroke, except for return of service, means a lost game. This will encourage you to take the net more. If you feel your volleys are too tentative, make any volley hit for a winner a game-winning shot.

3. For Better Overheads

Any lob allowed to bounce loses the game, and any player who retreats to the baseline after hitting an overhead loses the game. This drill will force you to try overheads on balls that Stan Smith might pass up, but the practice will do you good.

4. For More Consistent Serve

Play one serve on each point instead of two. This will force you to concentrate on getting the first serve in.

5. For Better Concentration

One interesting way of scoring to improve concentration is to agree that any three points won in a row represent a winning game. A variation is to agree that any three points lost, whether consecutive or not, while a player is serving lose the game. Both these variations will force you to concentrate more on each point.

6. For Better Lobs and Drop Shots

Any winning lob or drop shot wins the game.

There are also other possible scoring variations—some wildly ridiculous, others useful—but among the ones just mentioned you and an opponent should find several of particular benefit. If one of you tends to win all the time, one of these variations might make the competition closer and more exciting.

Ghost Doubles: Singles Practice for Better Doubles

by Bob Harman

A sizable number of tennis players excel at singles but are misfits on the doubles court. If you are one of them, you can help remedy the problem by playing what I like to call "Ghost Doubles." Ghost Doubles is doubles played by two players instead of four. In many ways, it is even more fun than singles; more important, it is an excellent way to improve your doubles play.

Here's how it works: You and your sparring partner simply agree that two quarters of the tennis court are out of bounds. Those quarters will be the sections which your nonexistent ghost partners would cover in a conventional doubles game. If you are serving from the forehand side of the court, your backhand side is just a black hole in space, and so is your opponent's. On the next point, when you move to serve from the left side, each player's forehand half of the court becomes taboo. Consequently, all shots must be aimed crosscourt— just as they are most of the time in regular doubles.

Do you see the logic of this? Think a moment about the usual positions of all four players in a doubles game at the instant when the player hits his serve. If the receiver returns it down the line, the server's partner at the net can easily step over and cut it off. That is why the receiver in doubles almost invariably angles his return into the server's half of the court: to keep it away from the server's partner in the other half. This is true whether the server is starting play for the right-hand or the left-hand side of the court.

When the serve is returned to him, the server also angles the next shot crosscourt. If he were to hit it straight, the receiver's partner in the forecourt could volley it out of reach.

In Ghost Doubles you simply agree that a ball hit into the ghost's half of the court is a lost point for the player who hits it. This means that both players must keep hitting crosscourt, as they would most of the time in an actual doubles game.

Ghost Doubles is a game in which you and your lone opponent play doubles style, using doubles-type strokes and tactics. You'll lob, dink and perhaps volley more than you could in singles. After your serve, you'll probably move straight ahead toward the net, remembering that you have only half of it to guard.

Whether you serve or receive, your objective in Ghost Doubles is the same as in normal doubles: to work your way toward the net in the half of the court from which you served or received, and then to make your opponent give you a rising ball which you can smack down at his feet or past him into the alley. Of course, the alley is considered within bounds in Ghost Doubles—on the "live" half of each court, that is.

You can play three sets of vigorous Ghost Doubles without getting any more tired than you would in one set of singles. You will get twice as much doubles practice as you would in conventional doubles because you serve every second game instead of every fourth,

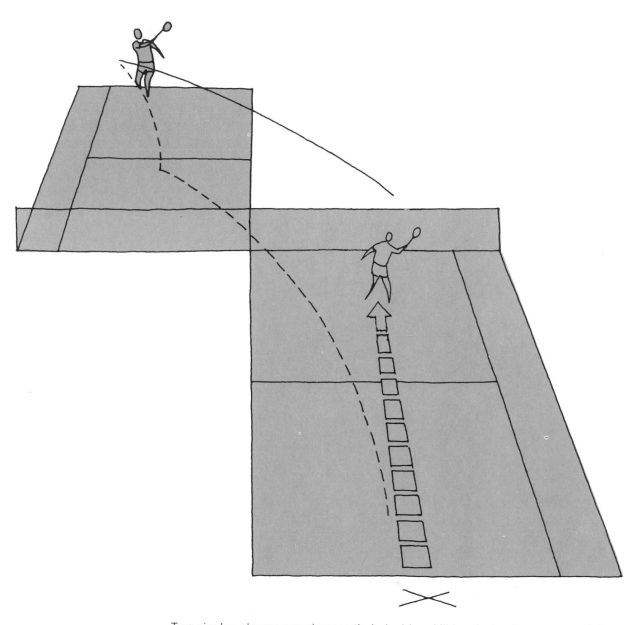

Two singles players can sharpen their doubles skill by playing the game as if there were an imaginary partner on each side. The pattern of play in the above illustration is totally crosscourt, since any ball hit down the line would be intercepted by the net "partner."

you receive all your opponent's serves instead of half of them and he hits all the balls toward your half of the court. You do more hitting and less standing around than you would in doubles. But you also will chug back and forth across the court much less than a singles player does.

It's as if you and your opponent each had a perfect, superhuman doubles partner who covers his own part of the court like a security blanket, never poaches on his teammate's sector, never growls or glares, never gets in the way. What could be more peaceful than playing doubles without a partner to plague you?

The next time you and a friend are playing by yourselves, instead of playing singles you might try Ghost Doubles. I'll bet you like it.

How to Practice the Lob
by Ron Holmberg

Players of every caliber spend hours and hours of practice time hitting forehands down the line or backhands crosscourt. How often do you see anyone practicing the lob? The overhead, yes, but seldom the lob.

Not practicing this shot, though, is a serious mistake. Every top player utilizes the lob both as an offensive weapon and as a defensive shot. And it is not a difficult shot to practice.

One way is to have a practice partner feed balls to you in all parts of the court. You can lob them back and he, in turn, can then practice his overhead. This is probably the best method of lob practice, since you have the actual feeling of a person at the net.

If another player isn't available, try to find a ball machine, preferably one that oscillates from side to side. Place it slightly inside the baseline and set it to fire balls deep into the opposite court.

A third method for working on the lob is to actually play points, games and sets with the understanding that you will hit the lob instead of a passing shot when your opponent comes to net. This will force you to hit good lobs, since your opponent knows what to expect.

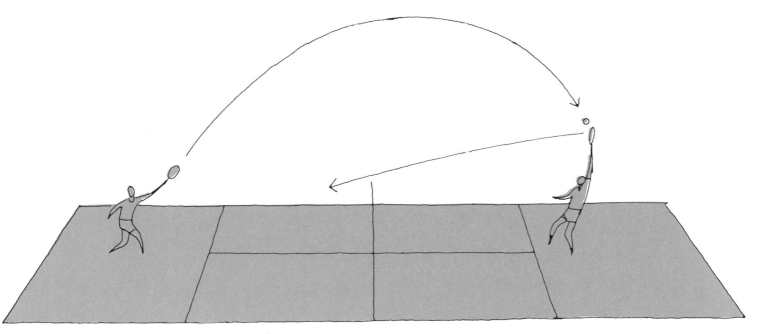

An easy way to work on the most neglected shot in tennis is to have a practice partner hit balls that you can lob. He, in turn, can then work on his overhead.

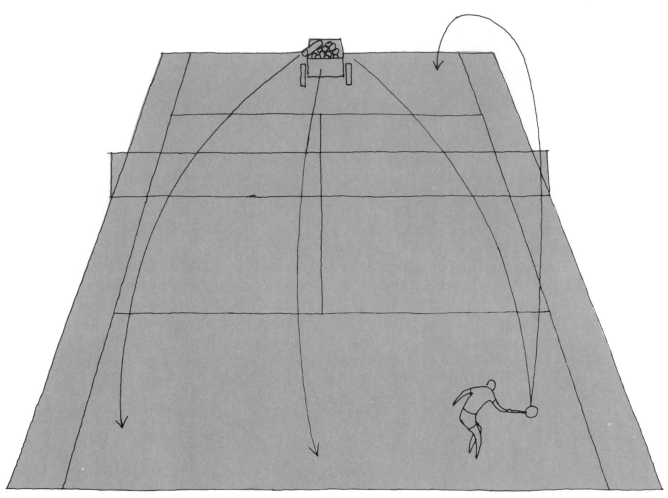

When practicing solo, place a ball machine—one that oscillates from side to side, if you can—just inside the baseline and set it to send balls deep into the other court.

Pauline Betz Addie demonstrates proper footwork for a backhand stroke.

Four Keys to Better Footwork
by Pauline Betz Addie

How often have you muffed an easy shot because you weren't in quite the right position at the right time? Maybe you practice your strokes against the backboard until they're near perfect, but do you ever check what your feet are doing before you hit the ball?

Chances are that you don't, and your footwork suffers accordingly. There's more to tennis footwork than merely running for the ball. Good footwork calls for the precision of a ballet dancer, the reflexes of a boxer and the timing of a basketball player.

Don't worry, though, if your footwork doesn't put you in this category. You can improve your footwork by doing a few simple drills you can practice by yourself and by learning a few basic movements that will cover virtually all your shots.

Before we look at the right way to move to the ball, I recommend that you practice the essential timing and weight shifts so vital to good footwork. Let's start with an exercise for the forehand.

Stand slightly behind the baseline with your left side to the net (if you play left-handed, you should reverse all my directions). Now toss the ball about a foot into the air slightly ahead of the baseline and far enough away from your body so that the racquet will have to make contact at arm's length. To get the timing right, say "up" as you toss the ball; "back" as you shift your weight to your right side and take your racquet back as the ball bounces; "swing" as you move to contact the ball.

Although your knees should be bent as you start to swing, straighten your front knee as you complete the swing. Your right toe should still be in contact with the ground, but your weight should have moved completely to your left side. Your knees, hips and shoulders should turn as though you were swinging at a baseball.

As you swing, your stance should be slightly closed, with your left foot extended a bit more than your right. It takes plenty of practice to toss the ball accurately for this exercise and even longer to coordinate the weight shift and swing. But persevere; before you can expect to polish your footwork, you have to develop timing.

Once your timing seems easy and natural, try throwing the ball higher and farther away from you so that you can move to hit it on its second bounce. You'll begin to realize the extreme importance of footwork in tennis. Aim for swift but short steps instead of taking one big step and lunging for the ball. You can't hit properly that way; your timing will be poor and your balance will, almost certainly, be disastrous.

For the right timing and weight shift on the backhand, simply follow a mirror image of the forehand. Practice the "up," "back" and "swing" rhythm as before.

These exercises will also teach you two important points: first, to stay away from the ball for an effective swing and second, to step in the direction in which you're hitting the ball to be sure you put your weight into the shot.

Footwork From Side to Side

Once your timing has been ironed out, we can begin to get ready for some tennis action.

First, let's consider the footwork you'll need to move sideways for your forehand and backhand. For both strokes, you should move to the ball with small steps that take you to a spot an arm's length behind the point at which you expect the bounce of the ball. When you arrive at this position, you should take another little step to permit you to pivot your weight onto your back foot before moving your weight and racquet through the shot.

Let's suppose you begin from the ready position in preparation for a forehand (see diagram 1). Start toward the ball on your right foot, slide your left foot up to the right, push off on the left foot and keep going with small steps until you arrive at an arm's length from the expected flight of the ball. For most shots, you'll have to take only a couple of steps to get to this point. As you arrive in the proper position, make your last step with your right foot a pivot to the right side. Then step across with your left foot into a slightly closed

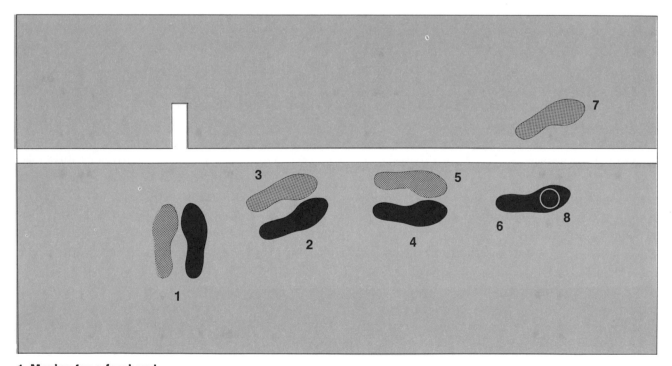

1. Moving for a forehand.
From the starting position (1), step out with your right foot (2), slide the left alongside (3) and take short steps (4, 5) until you arrive at about an arm's length from the flight of the ball (6). Then step out toward the net (7) and be prepared to pivot on your right foot (8) as you swing through the stroke. You'll finish with your weight on your forward foot.

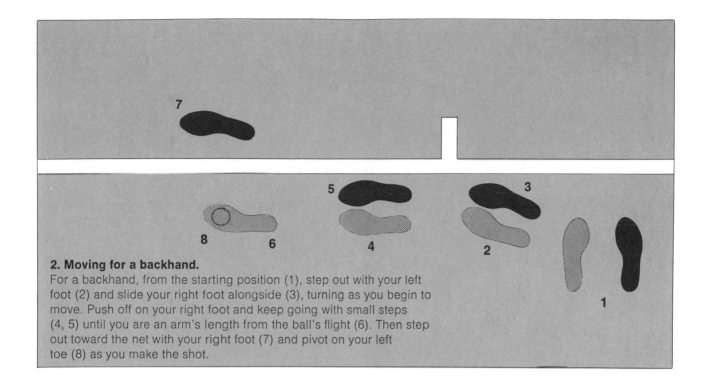

2. Moving for a backhand.
For a backhand, from the starting position (1), step out with your left foot (2) and slide your right foot alongside (3), turning as you begin to move. Push off on your right foot and keep going with small steps (4, 5) until you are an arm's length from the ball's flight (6). Then step out toward the net with your right foot (7) and pivot on your left toe (8) as you make the shot.

stance. Finally, transfer your weight and hit the ball.

Moving for a backhand often seems difficult for the average player. There is that moment of indecision when you wonder if you should run around and take the ball on your forehand. That moment's delay is usually followed by a frantic dash which gets you too close to the ball, and you muff the shot. The lesson is clear: make your decisions early and stick to them.

The backhand should mirror the forehand footwork (see diagram 2). Start with your left foot, slide the right foot up to the left, push off on the right and keep going until you are ready to pivot on the left side and swing your right foot over ready for the weight transfer and the actual shot.

Provided you have already mastered the pivot while standing still, you should be able to manage this step-and-turn movement quite easily. It helps to think of your turn as if you

were going to throw your racquet over the net with either a backhand or a forehand motion.

Footwork Up and Back

Of course, during a match, you have to move not only sideways for shots but up and back for short and deep balls as well. Moving toward the net in particular calls for early anticipation and accurate judgment of the point at which you stop a pivot in preparation for the shot. Again, the essential points are to use short steps and to turn before the bounce of the ball so that you'll have time to move your body into the shot. (See diagram 3, which shows how to move up for a backhand. In moving up for a forehand, the action is identical but in a mirror image of the diagram.)

If you have to retreat for a shot, start moving by the time the ball crosses the net or your feet won't be planted when you hit the ball

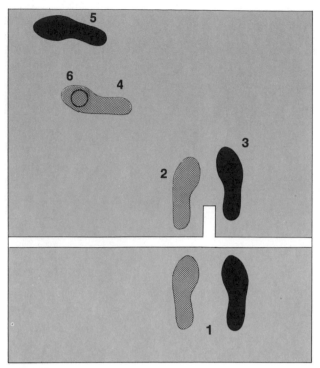

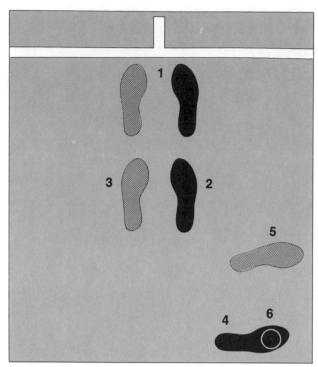

3. Getting up for the ball.
In moving up for a backhand, from the starting position (1), step off with your left foot (2), slide your right foot alongside (3) and then step and turn with your left (4). Now step toward the net with your right foot (5), keeping your weight on your left. As you make the shot, your weight will be transferred to your front foot and you'll pivot on your left (6).

4. Retreating for the ball.
When you retreat for a forehand, step back from the starting position (1) with your right foot (2) and bring your left foot alongside (3). Push off on your left foot and onto your right to begin your turn (4) and step over with your left (5) for a closed stance as you hit the shot. As you complete the shot, you'll pivot on your right foot (6) to complete the weight transfer.

(see diagram 4). Start on the outside foot (the right for a forehand), slide your left foot up to the right, push off on your left and pivot your weight back to the right side. (A mirror image shows you the footwork when moving back for a backhand.) The principles are the same as they are when you move sideways—"up," "back" and "swing."

As you work on improving your footwork, remember that great speed isn't really neces-

sary. You will need a quick start, small steps, effective weight transfer and good timing. You'll also need lots of practice before you can move about the court the way Muhammad Ali glides around the boxing ring.

Getting there is only part of the problem. When you have hit the ball, use that fancy footwork to get back to a good ready position for your next shot.

Chapter 20 Conditioning

A Conditioning Program for Every Player
by Harry Hopman

Are you discouraged or displeased with your progress in tennis? Do you want to improve your game dramatically? Well, you can. The way to do it can be summarized in three little words: Get in shape.

This may seem like very obvious advice, but you'd be surprised how many players ignore it. The average player's pregame preparation consists mainly of checking his tennis clothes, his sneakers and his racquet. The most exercise he gets, apart from the tennis, is the opening of a tennis can.

Well, tennis players pay for this lackadaisical approach, I assure you. It is particularly noticeable in the gradual decline of sharpness you see in the play of otherwise excellent doubles players once they get into a second hour of play. The errors mount—and the fault is almost always poor conditioning.

The pity of this situation is that it does not take all that much time to build up stamina. Just a few minutes a day of some very simple exercises and stroke practice can do wonders for your playing standard.

General Conditioning Exercises

Every morning, within a few minutes after rising, I do about four or five minutes of simple exercises. I repeat some of these exercises before retiring at night.

I begin with chest expanders. Expanders, which are inexpensive and can be bought in any sporting-goods store, are excellent for improving breathing and for maintaining good muscle tone in your shoulders, arms, wrists and fingers. They also help keep your chest out and your tummy in. My morning routine with expanders consists of pulling them slowly to full stretch of both arms 15 to 30 times, meanwhile breathing as deeply as possible. I do the same at night.

After using the expanders, I do a few situps and some toe touches. Don't worry on the toe touches if your first attempts are unsuccessful. Some mornings it takes longer to get limber. To help stomach muscles, I recommend pivoting from the hips, swinging the head and trunk of the body around—first to the right and then to the left. It is best to start with only five repetitions and build up slowly to as many as you can comfortably achieve. These pre-breakfast exercises will

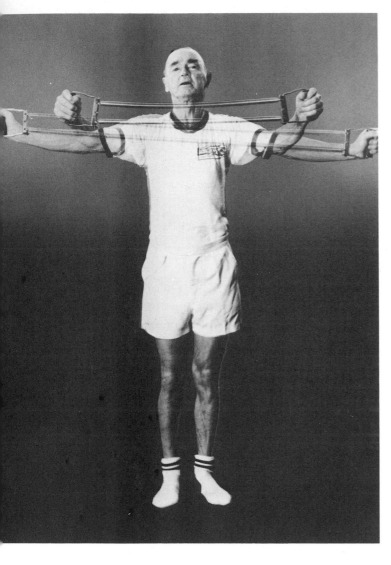

Harry Hopman demonstrates the use of a chest expander (left) and shows his form on sit-ups (top left), jogging (top right) and trunk pivoting (below).

cost you only five minutes a day. For myself, if the weather is suitable, I jog a mile or so. I don't think any conditioning activity is better for your tennis than running. It strengthens your legs and develops your stamina.

The exercises I've just mentioned are fine for general all-around conditioning. True, my exercise program isn't as rigorous as the programs many trainers recommend, but it does get rid of the creaks I would otherwise hear on the mornings when I start coaching.

Shadow Stroking

There are a number of exercises that have a direct effect on your tennis game. The best, to my mind, are those known as shadow stroking. Shadow stroking follows the same principle as shadowboxing. You simply go through the motions of stroking—with a racquet but no opponent and no ball to hit. You can do it outdoors or indoors. It can even be done in the dark—and at your own speed.

Your shadow-stroking routine should begin with ground strokes. Select a spot as your imaginary baseline and stand in the ready position, as if you were waiting for service. Then move three or four quick strides to stroke an imaginary ball on the forehand and, as the stroke is finished, instantly begin skipping back to the ready position. The sideways skip enables you to watch the imaginary ball and your opponent. Without waiting, repeat that stroke or dash the same three or four quick strides to your backhand side, play the stroke and skip back sideways again to the ready position. Repeat as often as time allows. If you can get a friend to call out the stroke you should hit, so much the better. It will introduce the element of surprise.

For the serve, practice your normal service motion but take your time between serves, making sure you are relaxed before beginning your next service. If you normally follow your serve to the net, go through that action. After a few strides, move sharply to the right or left for the imaginary receiver's return. Bend low, or perhaps reach wide and high, before continuing briskly on toward the net. Then move back to go through the motions of getting up to smash an imaginary lob.

Your shadow stroking can be as strenuous and as varied as you wish. And if you do it earnestly in conjunction with conventional exercises, you should see some startling improvement in your fitness and your performance on court.

For the Advanced Player

If you are an advanced player and would like to attain peak fitness, you can do so with a program similar to the one I used as coach of Australia's Davis Cup team for almost 20 years. This program has enabled such players as Ken Rosewall, Rod Laver, Frank Sedgman and Roy Emerson to stay in the best condition long past the recognized age of maximum fitness.

All of Australia's Davis Cup players have enjoyed the work involved in getting into peak physical shape, even though some of them were initially reluctant and, in fact, had to be pushed into realizing how it would improve their prospects of reaching the top. Here are some of the key exercises I used in training them:

The Double-knee Jump

Jump into the air as high as possible, keeping your head erect while your knees are

Paul Gerken demonstrates jog-sprints (top, left), the kangaroo hop (top, right), the double-knee jump (below, left) and the star jump (below right).

raised as close as possible to your chin. When you're doing this well, you will thump your chest with you kneecaps. Land lightly on your toes, ready to spring for the next leap. There should be no hesitations in a cycle of ten to fifty or even, once you've worked up to that level, one hundred jumps. But begin with only five repetitions and proceed slowly.

The Kangaroo Hop

Stand with your feet almost together and your hands hanging relaxed by your sides. Spring high and reach for the sky with your hands. Come down lightly on your toes, bend your knees and go down on your haunches. Rise ever so slightly off your toes and go down again to help you spring for the next leap upward. The hop should be a continuous movement done in cycles of ten jumps, or as many as you are able to complete without undue stress at one go. But again, begin with only five repetitions.

The Star Jump

Start with your feet together and your hands by your sides—facing, let's say, north. Jump quickly with your feet apart and arms raised to the shoulder level. Jump back to your original position. On the next jump, turn to the east or west and land facing that direction. Do one star jump to each of the four points of the compass. Next time around, do two jumps at each of the four compass points; next three, and then four. Reverse your direction, with four jumps at each compass point, then three and so on until you reach your original position. Repeat the complete cycle as many times as you can. However, this should be a "twinkle-toes" exercise; try not to lumber through it. It is better to cut the repetitions than to slow up and lose the quickness.

The Pulleys

A set of pulleys offers you an excellent way to strengthen your tennis strokes. Begin with a light weight, possibly five pounds. For a forehand, stand with your right shoulder (if you're right-handed) facing the pulleys and allow the weight on the end of the pulley to pull your arm well back while keeping your eyes frontward, as if following the flight of the ball. Then bend your knees and sweep the pulley out and around in a low stroking motion several times. Repeat with an imaginary ball at medium height and also with a higher-bouncing ball. With each sweep of the pulley, you should follow through just as you would with a normal stroke on the court. Try finishing your strokes with some shots down the line and some crosscourt. Repeat the exercise for the backhand. Don't let your head turn back toward the pulley as your arm stretches around before beginning your forward movement. Keep your eyes on that imaginary ball and feel the stretch on your arm and shoulder muscles.

Running

If you have time to run or jog, mix a run of about two miles with some jog-sprints, jogging 20 yards and sprinting 30 yards over a 150-yard course. Try to do your jogging off the road, since unyielding asphalt or cement can do more harm than good to your legs. Finally, make sure that you give yourself time to recover after each 150-yard dash.

Exercises Especially for Women

by Jane Boutelle

Women have turned to tennis in record numbers as a means of getting some exercise while they are having fun and being sociable at the same time. But even more than men, they have a tendency to rush out onto the court without any prior conditioning of their bodies. That's just asking for trouble.

A woman whose body is flabby and unfit will play more poorly than she should and may invite injury. A woman should follow sensible nutritional and health practices and engage in a regular regimen of exercises before trying to play tennis.

The conditioning program I recommend was drawn up specifically with women in mind, although there is no reason it cannot be performed by men if there are minor adjustments, such as more repetitions.

These exercises take into account the fact that the average female has a slighter body build than the male and different weight distribution. Most women have small shoulders and a more flexible pelvis than a man's. On the tennis court, this means that a woman cannot smash an overhead as readily from the backcourt as a man; on the other hand, she is able to skip or slide more easily from side to side. My conditioning program recognizes these differences.

For all of the exercises illustrated here, start by lying on your back with your knees flexed above your hips. Your right knee should be over your right hip and the left knee over the left hip. The lower legs should be parallel to the floor, with your toes pointing to the ceiling. Your arms should be fully extended, palms up, parallel to your trunk. Keep your back and shoulders firmly against the floor throughout the exercises.

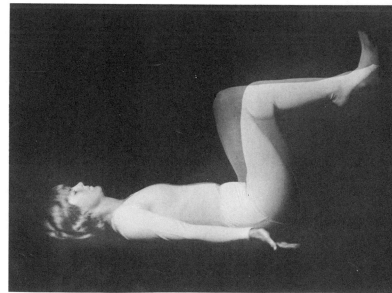

Inhale deeply, point your toes away from the body and pull your knees toward their respective shoulder joints, as pro star Tory Fretz does here. Keep your lower back on the floor and your knees parallel to the floor. Exhale slowly and push back to the starting position. The first week, try this abdominal tightener ten times, increasing gradually as best you can.

Stretch your left leg upward so that the left ankle is over the left hip. At the same time, flex your right knee fully and bring the right toes down to touch the floor under or in front of your right hip. Breathing deeply, slowly alternate the position of your legs. Try ten alterations at first, increasing gradually later.

Inhale deeply, then exhale and push your lower legs toward the ceiling. The soles of your feet should be parallel to the ceiling, and the ankles over their respective hip joints. Slowly exhale, while pointing your toes toward the ceiling and stretching your legs. Inhale, flex your knees and bring your lower legs back to the starting position. Finally, exhale and flex your ankles so that they return to the starting position. Repeat this four-part exercise five times.

Stretch your left leg upward so that the left ankle is over the left hip. Point the left toes toward the ceiling with your left knee straight. Now flex the right knee fully and place the sole of your right foot on the floor under or in front of your right hip. Breathing deeply, slowly rotate the left ankle to the right and complete a full circle five times. On the next five rotations, turn the leg as well as the ankle. Reverse the position of your legs and do this exercise with the right leg extended. Then repeat the entire exercise.

How a Pro Stays in Condition
by John Alexander

Professional men's tennis has long since passed the point at which the gifted player could get by on his talents alone. Nowadays the top players are true athletes, and virtually all of us take care to stay in prime physical shape during the season.

For me, staying in top condition means a regular exercise and tennis-practice program plus a diet low in carbohydrates. During the off-season, when I play only occasionally, my fitness level declines and my weight inevitably goes up to around 200 pounds from its normal level of about 180 pounds. So a few weeks before the World Championship Tennis circuit starts, I begin daily workouts at the gym near my home in Sydney, Australia.

Under the supervision of an instructor, I do about 45 minutes of intensive exercises while he acts as a kind of drill sergeant to make me keep at it without letup. We generally start off with some gentle bending and stretching exercises to warm up my muscles. I accompany these exercises with rhythmic deep breathing to help increase my lungs' oxygen capacity.

When I am sufficiently warmed up, we progress to tougher exercises which are designed to strengthen the stomach and leg muscles. These consist of a sequence of double-knee jumps, toe touching in midair, toe-touching sit-ups and so on.

I also do a lot of what I call "animal" exercises while hanging from a horizontally suspended ladder. That involves moving along the ladder while hanging by my hands and "hopping" from rung to rung. This is excellent for strengthening the arm, chest and stomach muscles for overhead work. But these kinds of exercises are very demanding physically, so I do not recommend them for anyone who is not in unusually good shape.

My workouts are interspersed with short sprints and other rapid-movement exercises. There is no break for the entire 45 minutes to an hour. Later in the day, I'll go out onto the court and practice for three or four hours—which, besides helping develop my game, also serves to strengthen my leg muscles and build up my stamina.

Today, when I'm on tour I play virtually every day, which means I don't need to engage in quite such a vigorous exercise program. Still, I take the time to do sit-ups, toe touching and some jogging daily. And I take special care to watch my diet, since I usually live in hotels when I'm on the circuit. I hold down on sugar, potatoes and bread, and eat lots of steaks and salads. I find that I can control my weight pretty easily just by being careful with my diet, which makes it easier to stay in shape.

The top players appear to be sufficiently dedicated to the game to have regular exercise programs of their own. It seems to be easier for the natural athletes, men like Roger Taylor, John Newcombe, Stan Smith and Arthur Ashe, to keep in shape than for players like, say, Ken Rosewall and Cliff Drysdale. Although he doesn't like it known, Rosewall works very hard at conditioning—a fact that I discovered after talking to his milkman back in Sydney. Apparently, Rosewall runs every day around dawn and the only person who has seen him is the milkman!

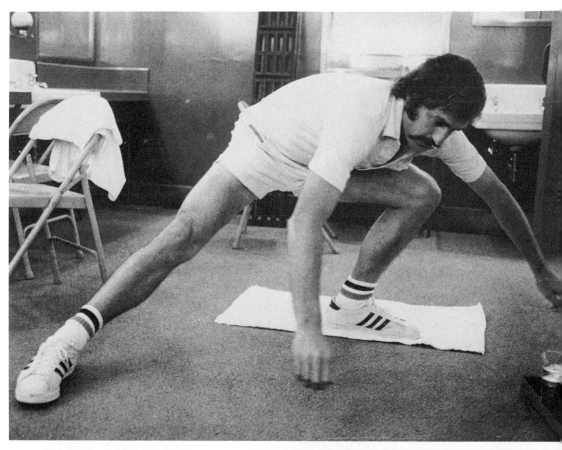

Both John Newcombe (top) and Stan Smith (lower) keep in peak match fitness with daily exercise programs.

Art Credits: